Legends of Country Music

Waylon Jennings

An unauthorized fan tribute

By: James Hoag

Paperback Edition

Manufactured in the United States of America

Also by James Hoag

The following are available in paperback.

Legends of Rock & Roll Volume 1 - The Fifties

Legends of Rock & Roll Volume 2 - The Sixties

Legends of Rock & Roll Volume 3 - The Seventies

Legends of Rock & Roll

Neil Diamond
Queen
Eagles
The Beatles
John Lennon
Paul McCartney
George Harrison
Ringo Starr

Legends of Country Music

Reba McEntire
Garth Brooks
Willie Nelson
Johnny Cash
George Jones
Merle Haggard

(All available at Amazon.com)

TABLE OF CONTENTS

INTRODUCTION

I've never seen Waylon Jennings in person, but I've heard his music, and I've seen him and his pals on TV. I grew up with rock-and-roll and didn't find country music until about 1980 when I met a guy who worked as a disc jockey at a local country radio station. He and I became close friends, probably the best friend I have ever had in my life, and he introduced me to country music. I've never looked back.

When you write a series of books called "The Legends of Country Music," you better be sure that the people you write about are truly legends. Of course, what a legend is to one person may not be considered a legend to another, so you're stuck with my interpretation of the term. This is the seventh book I have written about a person I consider to be a country music legend, and I think I'm truly on the mark when it comes to Waylon Jennings.

His career in country music is hard to beat. He recorded 60 albums and has had sixteen number one songs on the country music charts. He was born in Texas, lived as hard as he worked, and eventually married four times. He died in 2002 in Chandler, Arizona of an illness related to diabetes.

His career spanned five decades, and he has been inducted into the Country Music Hall of Fame. If you enjoy country music, I bet that you like Waylon Jennings. Come with me as I examine his life and loves and, most importantly, his music. I present to you: Waylon Jennings.

1 - GROWING UP IN TEXAS

Waylon Jennings grew up just outside Littlefield, Texas. Littlefield is a small town. The population was just over 6000 in 2010 but in 1937, when Waylon was born, it was about 3600. Littlefield was then and is still to this day an area where cotton is grown. And that's what the Jennings family did: they picked cotton. That was their main livelihood. The Jennings lived about six or seven miles outside of Littlefield on a small farm.

The Jennings worked as what was called "Subsistence Farmers." This means they grew just enough food for their own family and nothing more. They lived on the property of a man named J. W. Bittner and picked cotton for him when it came into season. The family lived in a two-room house (probably more of a shack) with a dirt floor. They shared those two rooms with uncles, aunts, and cousins. A total of twelve people lived there.

On June 15, 1937, Waylon's Mama was nine months pregnant. As she walked up to the main house owned by Mr. Bittner, out popped Waylon. His mother was Lorene Beatrice Shipley, and his father was William Albert Jennings. No mention of the birth was made in any of the local newspapers. I'm assuming a legal birth certificate was created, but that was the only thing that documented the birth of Waylon Jennings.

They originally named him Wayland but, one day, a Baptist preacher stopped by the house and commented that he was so pleased to see they had named their son after the wonderful Wayland Baptist University in Plainview, Texas (at that time, it was just called Wayland College). The Jennings were religious people, but they weren't Baptists (they were Church of Christ), so Mama changed the spelling of his name to Waylon and so it has been known all his life. Waylon says his birth certificate still has the original spelling.

The main activity growing up was picking cotton, and Waylon picked cotton until he was sixteen. Then, one day, he decided that he'd had enough, laid down the sack, and never picked cotton again. Even though the family stayed in the Littlefield area, they did move a lot when Waylon was growing up. The homes gradually got better and better and by the time Waylon was in grammar school, they moved into a home that had real wood floors and indoor plumbing. That was the first time anyone in the family had experienced that.

Eventually, Dad put together enough money to open a produce store in town. This was the big time for the family and allowed them to buy some things that they might not have afforded before. One thing they could get was a guitar. When Waylon was eight-years-old, his mother sat him down with the guitar and taught him how to play "Thirty Pieces of Silver." This is an old gospel song which you can find on YouTube by Hank Williams. Waylon signed up for some guitar lessons from a local teacher, but the two of them didn't get along and, soon, Waylon quit the lessons and decided he would just teach himself to play.

Waylon's musical interests came from a lot of places. Like most people in the south in that era, they would sit around the radio in the evening and listen to the Grand Ole Opry coming from Nashville, Tennessee. He started to get interested in certain singers and enjoyed listening to them. Some of his early influences in music were Bob Wills, Ernest Tubb, Hank Williams, Carl Smith, and, of course, Elvis Presley, who influenced everyone in the Fifties. He picked up the blues from visiting a local black nightclub called Jaybird's Dew Drop Inn. It was probably on the outskirts of Littlefield, as a Google search does not show that it exists today. Waylon says he was the only white boy allowed into the Dew Drop Inn.

Soon, Waylon was taking his guitar out in public and playing for people other than his family. He played for the local Jaycees and the Lions Club. It was a great experience. When he was about ten-years-old, he won his first talent contest. Because of that, he was invited to play on television station KLBK-TV in Lubbock, Texas which was about 30 miles southeast of Littlefield. He sang the Carl Smith song "Hey Joe," and he won a watch. Waylon says it wasn't until they got home that he discovered that the watch didn't work. It was completely empty inside, so the family drove back to Lubbock and demanded a working watch. They got one, and Waylon was pleased.

When he was twelve, he auditioned for a spot on a weekly radio show on KVOW-AM radio in Littlefield. He played the guitar, and some of his friends made up the rest of the band. KVOW is long gone from Littlefield and today is KZZN. His experience playing once a week on the radio gave him the confidence to put some guys together and form his own band which he called the Texas Longhorns.

Waylon and school just didn't get along and, by the time he was sixteen, he had quit. He just couldn't see that it helped him that much. His life was hanging with his friends and smoking on the nearest corner. When I picture Waylon and his friends, I get a vision of John Travolta and the gang from the movie *Grease*. The movie takes place about the time Waylon was in high school.

On Christmas Eve, 1955, Waylon married Maxine Carroll Lawrence. There is very little online about Maxine. She was probably born about the same time as Waylon since they attended high school together and were in the same grade. To call her his high school sweetheart is being a little optimistic. They went together, spent their time necking in the back seat of his car and, when she missed a period and thought she was pregnant, the two of them went to Clovis, New Mexico, where a local preacher married them. They went to New Mexico to get married because New Mexico didn't require a blood test and Texas did. The next day, Maxine's period started, so the whole thing was a false alarm. However, they were still married and would remain so long enough to have four kids. Those were Terry, born in 1957, Julie, born in 1958, Buddy, born in 1960, and Deanna. I cannot find a birth year for Deanna. MyHeritage.com says she was born in 1964, but that seems very late to me since by that time he had been married to wife number two for two years. He divorced Maxine in 1962. He married his second wife in 1962, so it must have been before that. He would eventually have four wives. Every record I have found says she was born in 1964. It could just be that he cheated on his second wife with his first wife.

2 - BUDDY HOLLY

Since he was no longer going to high school, Waylon needed a job. After a couple of menial jobs with lumber companies that didn't work out, he got on as a disk jockey for KVOW, the Voice of Lamb County, 1490 on your AM-radio dial. He worked from four in the afternoon until ten at night, and he played mostly country music. He would bring his guitar to the station and, from time-to-time, he would play and sing on the air. The people liked it. Then he discovered rock-and-roll and started playing artists like Elvis Presley and Little Richard. His boss wasn't too happy about that, but Waylon didn't care.

He says he got to meet Elvis in 1954 when he came to Lubbock to perform. Elvis sang his hits of the day like "That's All Right Mama" and "Blue Moon of Kentucky." When Waylon started playing that kind of music on KVOW, he got in trouble with the boss, but Waylon didn't care. He went on doing it anyway. Waylon says that one night, he played two Little Richard songs back-to-back, and the station owner fired him.

His hero at this time was Sonny Curtis. Curtis could really play the guitar, and Waylon was in awe of him. Waylon worked and worked trying to play as good as Curtis. Curtis was born in Meadow, Texas, which is only about an hour's drive from Littlefield, so he and Waylon would hang out when they could.

Meadow Texas, Littlefield Texas, and Lubbock Texas formed a triangle. Each was about 45-50 miles from the other two. Since Waylon couldn't go to the local radio station, having been fired, he and Curtis would hang out in Lubbock at station KDAV-AM. Lubbock was where it was happening anyway. Elvis came through Lubbock as did many other performers that Waylon got to meet. He and Sonny Curtis would sit in the KDAV radio station and play together while a crowd of onlookers would watch and listen from outside. Besides the station, they hung out at a Lubbock restaurant called Avenue Q, and this is where he met several other guitar players who lived in Lubbock.

One guitar player in particular was making some waves in Lubbock. His name was Charles "Buddy" Holly. He was a year older than Waylon and had a two-man band called Buddy and Bob. As time went on, Buddy Holly's band grew, and members were added to it. Those members would soon become known as The Crickets and eventually Waylon would get a job playing with the Crickets as would Sonny Curtis. Buddy Holly got a contract with Decca Records and so he went off to Nashville to start recording. Waylon still had some growing up to do, and he needed to learn his craft a little more, before he could leave Texas behind.

A new station came into Lubbock, and Waylon went to work for them. They were KLLL (or, as they were known locally, K-triple-L), and Waylon had a great time working for them. They gave him the morning shift which meant he had to fire up the transmitter every morning to get the station on the air. Waylon says there was many a morning when he would sleep in and be late for work. He describes driving down the back roads of Texas at 80 miles an hour listening to dead air coming over the radio instead of his broadcast. It's a wonder they didn't fire him, but he was, otherwise, a good D.J. and so he kept the job.

Waylon started writing songs while he was working as a disc jockey. Sometimes, he would have his guitar, and he would play and sing over the air. He got his live experience playing a local bar called The Cotton Club. I think the bar is still there in Lubbock (they have a Facebook page). In the late Fifties, it was the type of bar where they had to put chicken netting in front of the band because the patrons would throw empty beer bottles at them. Waylon cut his teeth playing at the Cotton Club. Elvis Presley played there in 1955 when he was in town to promote a local car dealer.

Waylon said that he thought that since Buddy Holly had "made it," why couldn't someone else, like him, make it as well. Thus, he kept writing and kept practicing. One day, Buddy came back to Lubbock and looked up his old friend. He was thinking about starting a record label and wanted Waylon to be the first to record on the new label. Buddy took Waylon to Clovis, New Mexico to Norman Petty's recording studios and there they recorded Waylon's first record, a tune called "Jole Blon." "Jole Blon" is an old Cajun waltz which dates back to the 1800's and was recorded for the first time in 1929 by a family group, the Breaux Brothers. They put words to the music and expanded on the song a little and "Jole Blon" has become a standard of American music.

This was Waylon's first record. It is significant because while he does the vocal, Buddy Holly plays the guitar and King Curtis is on tenor sax. It was recorded on the Brunswick label, which was Buddy's label at the time. The record was released but didn't chart anywhere. That makes it one of the rarest records around these days.

Waylon wanted to record more, but Buddy had to complete a tour he was contracted to fulfil. That tour was called The Winter Dance Party.

James Hoag

3 - "THE DAY THE MUSIC DIED"

The original Crickets were with Buddy Holly when "Jole Blon" was recorded but while they were in Lubbock, they got into a big fight over the pay they were getting (or not getting), and the Crickets went on strike. Therefore, Buddy and Waylon went to New York in an effort to start Waylon's career. Buddy had, by this time, married Maria Elena, and they were living in New York. While there, Buddy introduced Waylon to many people and to the life of being a recording artist. Waylon was in awe of it all.

Since the Crickets were still in Lubbock and still feuding with Buddy Holly, Buddy put together a new band. The first person he picked was Waylon, who was given two weeks to learn how to play the bass guitar. He did it. The others were Tommy Allsup on guitar and drummer Carl "Goose" Bunch. Although the three newcomers were not the Crickets, all the promotion had already been done listing the headlining act as Buddy Holly and the Crickets, so the three new guys became the Crickets. Also going were the supporting acts: Dion and the Belmonts, J.P. Richardson (known as the Big Bopper), Ritchie Valens, and Frankie Sardo. Waylon said that Sardo was the worst singer he had ever heard. Buddy was certainly the headliner. Dion had only had a couple hits as had Valens and Richardson, who was famous for the party song "Chantilly Lace."

The tour was a disaster right from the beginning. They were all crammed into an old bus with a broken heater, and this was January and February in the Midwest. The tour started on January 23, 1959 at George Devine's Ballroom in Milwaukee, Wisconsin. From there, they went to Kenosha, Wisconsin and then to Mankato, Minnesota. The tour continued in mostly small towns in Wisconsin and Minnesota. Experiencing temperatures as low as -25 °F, the trip was miserable. They were so cold that Carl Bunch, Buddy's drummer, got frostbite on his feet and had to leave the tour on the first of February. This, undoubtedly, saved his life. When Bunch left the tour, Richie

Page | 15

Valens stepped in and played drums for the next couple of venues. Since all of the acts were basically vocal groups, Waylon, Tommy Allsup, and Carl Bunch were the band for all of them. That way, they could get by without extra musicians.

On February 2, 1959, they stopped at the Surf Ballroom in Clear Lake. They completed the performance and then were scheduled to be driven by bus to Moorhead, Minnesota the next day. I don't think I-94 existed in 1959, so this was about a 400-mile trip over snowy two-lane roads in sub-zero weather with no heater. Buddy had had enough. He hired a small plane and a local pilot, Roger Peterson, to fly him and two others to Moorhead. Originally, the two others were to be Tommy Allsup and Waylon Jennings from his band (Carl Bunch was still in the hospital with frostbite). However, J.P. Richardson had the flu and came up to Waylon during a break in the concert and asked Waylon if he wouldn't mind taking the bus so Richardson could fly. Waylon Jennings was just so happy to be a part of it all that he readily agreed, so The Big Bopper took one of the two available seats. Richie Valens got together with Tommy Allsup, and they tossed a coin to see who would take the last seat. Tommy said tails, the coin said heads, and Ritchie won the seat.

The band would have to ride the bus while the three stars would fly in the plane. As they parted company, Buddy jokingly told Waylon, "I hope your ol' bus freezes up!" Waylon retorted, "Well, I hope your ol' plane crashes." That remark would haunt Waylon Jennings for the rest of his life.

The plane, a Beechcraft Bonanza, took off from Mason, Iowa airport in heavy snow a little after midnight on the early morning of February 3, 1959. The plane was only in the air about five minutes when it crashed in a farmer's field close to Clear Lake. All four people on the plane were killed instantly. The pilot, Roger Peterson, literally flew the plane into the ground in the snow storm. It was later learned that Paterson was not instrument trained and had no business flying in snow. They also determined that he knew something bad was happening as he tried to land the plane. He took the snow off of a roof of a house and then crashed into the ground.

Since the plane did not catch on fire when it crashed, the wreckage was not found until dawn.

There were rumours that J.P. Richardson had walked away from the crash site alive because his body was discovered over 50 feet from the wreckage. No one knew for sure. CSI work wasn't as good in those days as it is today. He could have been thrown in the crash. Many years later, an autopsy was done on Richardson, and it was determined that almost every bone in his legs had been broken. There is no way he could have walked away from the crash.

If you're ever in Iowa and want to visit the site, it's easy to find. The crash site is in a corn field one half mile from the intersection of Gull Ave and 333 Street, three miles north of Clear Lake, Iowa. You can take exit 197 from I-35. You'll know you're in the right place when you see a statue of a big pair of black horn-rimmed glasses.

The rest of the group did not know what had happened until they got to Moorhead, Minnesota the next morning and were notified of the tragedy. The news reported that Buddy Holly "and his band" had been killed and, for several hours, Waylon's mother thought he was dead. It was only later in the afternoon of the third of February that Waylon thought to call home and tell his mother that he was all right. They had a show to do in Moorhead and now they were missing the headlining acts. Consequently, Waylon Jennings went on and sang lead for some of Buddy's songs. They also recruited a young unknown man from Fargo, Minnesota who sounded like Buddy Holly to step in and replace him. That young man was Bobby Vee. This kick started Vee's career, and he had several hits after this point.

Losing Buddy Holly had a profound impact on Waylon. Buddy was his one and only friend in the music business. When it came time to be paid for the tour, the business people tried to short the remaining guys by saying that since the three stars were all dead, they didn't have to pay as much to the rest. Waylon just about came unglued and threatened them saying he would do more damage than the amount they owed him. Therefore, they relented and paid the guys what they had coming to them. Waylon came very close to leaving the music business after that. They finished the tour, and Waylon went home, intending to never go on the road like that again.

Buddy Holly's funeral was held on February 7th at the Temple Baptist Church in Lubbock. Officiating at the service was Ben D. Johnson, who was the pastor who had married Buddy and Maria Elena just six months before. Pallbearers were members of his original Crickets group: Niki Sullivan, Jerry Allison, and Joe B. Mauldin. Bob Montgomery (his old friend from school), Sonny Curtis, and Phil Everly (a friend he had toured with - and half of the Everly Brothers) also took part.

The new version of the Crickets, including Waylon Jennings, could not attend as they were still on the road with The Winter Dance Party Tour. Buddy was buried in the Lubbock City Cemetery. His headstone shows the correct spelling of his name (he was born Charles Hardin Holley) and a carving of a Fender Stratocaster guitar for which he was known.

Maria Elena also did not attend the funeral and has never been to the cemetery to view the grave. Maria learned of Buddy's death from the media. It was all over the radio on the morning of February 3rd. The shock of hearing about his death caused what doctors call "psychological trauma," and she lost Buddy's baby that she was carrying. It is said that because of this incident, a new policy was enacted in the United States which said that, with a violent death like this, the victim's name would not be released until the family is notified.

The very next day after the tragedy, Eddie Cochran wrote and recorded a tribute to the three lost stars called "Three Stars." A couple months later, Tommy Dee also released "Three Stars," and the people liked this version better as it went to number 11 on the Billboard charts.

Twelve years later, Don McLean recorded the famous "American Pie" or "The Day the Music Died." This was in 1972, and it seemed to emphasize the loss of America's innocence. I can remember hearing "American Pie" and wondering what it all meant. McLean had the number one song of the year with "American Pie," and we still occasionally hear the song today.

I have always wondered what happened to the tour after losing its three headliners. Well, the tour went on until February 15th. Frankie Sardo, Dion and the Belmonts, and the (fake) Crickets all finished the tour. The Crickets added Ronnie Smith to sing vocals. Bobby Vee and the Shadows sang for the concert on February 3rd. Jimmy Clanton, Fabian, and Frankie Avalon were added as headliners for the tour. The show must go on.

4 - RISING OUT OF THE ASHES

When the tour was over, Waylon Jennings went home. He was a mess. He felt like his career was over before it had even started. He went back to work at KLLL, but his heart wasn't in it. He was listless on the air and soon the managers had to take him aside and ask him if he really wanted this job or maybe he should do something else.

At this time, he was still married to Maxine. They had two kids in 1959 and, a year later, she gave birth to their third, whom they called Buddy. Guess who he was named after? Later, people would say that Buddy was the spitting image of his dad. Waylon was really struggling. He worked at KLLL and KDAV, but it didn't feel like he fit in anywhere. He tried other stations, but they didn't work either. He was seriously having trouble putting food on the table and paying the rent.

Waylon felt like he needed a change of scenery, and that came through Maxine's father. He lived in Arizona and so the Jennings family went to visit him. Maxine's sister also lived nearby, and they got to have a little family reunion. Waylon really liked Arizona and, after several trips back and forth, settled there. There was nothing much for him in Texas anymore, anyway.

Arizona was like a shot in the arm for Waylon. He liked the mountains, the scenery, the clubs, and, most importantly, he felt motivated to get back to what he did best: write new music, play the guitar, and sing. He met a man named Jim Garshow who was working at the same radio station in Coolidge, Arizona where Waylon was working. They took an instant disliking to each other. They had to work together, but the tension became so high that, finally, they just sat down and each asked the other why they didn't like the other. Turns out, it was nothing. They laughed about it, got over it, and started working fine together. Waylon says they were friends for the rest of his life.

He also met a fellow named Tom Haley who was a slick salesman. He went to drive-ins around the area and convinced them to have Waylon and his band play a fifteen minute set on the roof of the refreshment building during intermission at the drive-in. Waylon brought his band to the drive-in, and Jim Garshow would do the talking and introducing the group. Waylon and the band would play for about fifteen minutes while the next movie was being queued up. This was a cool way to make a living, and Waylon and the band travelled all over the west, stopping at every little town that had a drive-in. That was fun for a while but soon got tiring. Tom Haley was a nice guy but a mean drunk. One time, in Idaho, when he was drunk, he pulled a gun on Waylon. Waylon said, "The hell with this" and quit. He and one of his band members, Billy Joe Stevens, left Haley in Blackfoot, Idaho and headed south where they stopped in Salt Lake City, Utah.

They asked for work at a local club, and the woman running the club was Lynne Mitchell. She not only hired Waylon, but she became his second wife.

5 - THE WAYLORS

Maxine didn't enjoy living in Arizona (even though this is where much of her family lived). Waylon was gone all of the time, and she was left to raise the three kids (and there was one more on the way). Waylon was so busy, he hardly noticed that she had left and gone back to Lubbock. They were divorced in 1962. The exact date doesn't seem to be known, but it had to have been before December 10, 1962, since that is the day he married his second wife, Lynne Mitchell.

Waylon moved to Phoenix and created his own band. He was hoping to record one day, and he needed a band to do that. He called the band, The Waylors, which is a fun twist on his name. The band kind of grew over time. Waylon started out working at a bar called Wild Bill's, but Bill fired him, so he went to a place called Frankie's. It was there that a guy named Jerry Groop asked if he could sit in and play with the band. He played the guitar left-handed. Soon after that, his cousin, Ed Metsendorf, also showed up at Frankie's and soon he was playing with the band as well. He was also left-handed. Waylon recalls that there he was between two guys playing their guitars left-handed. It looked like Waylon was the one that was out of place. Even so, they got along, and Jerry and Ed were the start of the Waylors. Ed didn't stay long with the Waylors and soon went his own way. Waylon replaced him with Paul Foster, who played bass and who stayed with the band for as long as they were in Phoenix.

By now, Lynne Mitchell had left Salt Lake City and her husband and had moved to Phoenix. She was taken with Waylon even though she was eight years older than him and was married. She saw nothing wrong with following Waylon to Arizona. She soon divorced her husband and moved in with Waylon (not necessarily in that order).

Waylon's job in Phoenix got more permanent when a fellow named Jimmy D. Musiel (called J.D. by all his friends) moved to town and began building a two-story nightclub called JD's. There would be music upstairs and downstairs, and he invited Waylon and the Waylors to be a part of it. Waylon was suddenly the headliner and while he liked to play in the style of Johnny Cash, he soon realized that guitars were not enough. He needed a drummer, so he recruited a fellow named Richie Albright to play drums, and the Waylors were complete. Of the three members of the Waylors, besides Waylon himself, Richie Albright was the only one to stay with Waylon as long as there was a band. Richie was still with him when he died.

A friend Waylon had known back in Lubbock, Texas, came to town one day in 1963 and asked Waylon if he might help finish some songs he had written. Waylon agreed. His name was Don Bowman, and he used to work at KLLL in Lubbock. In the late Fifties or early Sixties, he moved to San Diego, California where he wrote songs. He didn't exactly start the world on fire, but he had some success. He wrote a song for Homer and Jethro that was a moderate hit. Later, he would have a hit of his own called "Chit Atkins, Make Me a Star." ("Chit" is purposely misspelled. The record is supposed to be a joke.) It hit the Top 40, but that was about it for Bowman.

At the time Bowman came to Phoenix, he was writing songs, or at least parts of songs, and he wanted Waylon's help to finish some of them. I probably wouldn't even mention him, except he had written part of a song which would later be a big hit for Waylon, "Just to Satisfy You." But, even more important, Don introduced Waylon to a record executive out in Los Angeles named Jerry Moss. Moss was the "M" of A&M Records, the "A," of course, being Herb Albert. Alpert was just starting out and had only one hit under his belt, "The Lonely Bull."

Albert and Moss decided they needed some new blood for their new record label and asked Waylon to sign on with them with the promise of at least one single. Consequently, Waylon travelled to L.A. and tried to fit in with the big-leaguers. It was a losing battle. They wanted Waylon to be something he wasn't. Herb Albert wanted a crooner, like Al Martino. Waylon was more like Flatt and Scruggs (his words). The first record Waylon recorded was "Love Denied," written by Bill Tilghman and, to capitalize on Waylon's fame with Buddy Holly, they put "Rave On" on the B-side. He then recorded two more records while he was in L.A., and A&M released them through the year of 1964. They got a little airplay but not enough sales to hit the charts. Eventually, Waylon went back to Arizona, his tail tucked firmly between his legs.

He knew he was doing something right because the crowds at JD's were enthusiastic and loud. They enjoyed the Waylors, so why wouldn't the rest of the country? In the fall of 1964, Waylon recorded his first album, called *Waylon at JD's*. It sold out of the club as a souvenir record and wasn't released outside of Phoenix for many years. It contained all of the music which Waylon was famous for at the club. He could do a pretty good imitation of Roy Orbison (high pitched singing and all), so he liked to perform "Crying," and that went on the album. He had to do a Buddy Holly song, so "It's So Easy" was recorded. In 1963, Buck Owens recorded "Love's Gonna Live Here" and, to stay close to his country roots, Waylon included it. Waylon recorded twelve songs for the album, and it sold pretty well out of the club. The album was recorded in such a way that everyone who heard it thought it was a live album when, in fact, it was all done in the studio.

While Waylon was struggling to get noticed in the music world, things were not that great at home. He and Lynne were like two tigers in cage. The fighting was almost constant. I'm surprised they stayed together as long as they did. Lynne got pregnant and while that should be a time of celebration, the doctors discovered she had nephritis, which is a kidney disease. This meant that they had to choose between

Lynne's life and the baby's life. Both could not live. Therefore, Lynne was forced to have an abortion to save her life. This was a crushing blow to Lynne. She wanted a baby, but it didn't look like it was possible, so they decided to adopt. That worked really well. Through friends, they found a girl who was expecting and couldn't keep the baby, so they arranged to adopt the child. It was a little girl, and they named her Tomi Lynne. This was not Waylon's first child (he had had four with Maxine), but there was something special about Tomi. Waylon says that when Tomi looked at him, it was as if she was really seeing him. Things looked good for once but then Maxine sent their four kids to live with Waylon.

The arrival of the other four kids would eventually end the marriage between Waylon and Lynne. Lynne hated the four that were not hers and was fairly mean to them. Finally, Waylon had had enough and sent the kids back. Then he went to Lynne and told her it was over between them. I'm not sure exactly when this happened, but Lynne filed for divorce on January 11, 1967 and soon it was official. The grounds for divorce were listed as "excesses, outrages, and cruelty."

Waylon was not one to let grass grow under his feet. Before he and Lynne had even broken up, he was with his next wife. Her name was Barbara Rood and, she came from a wealthy family. Waylon was taken by her (and she, him) when they first met. This was several years before his official divorce with Lynne. When Lynne walked out, Waylon went right to Barbara. They were together until about 1968, when that relationship fell apart just like the others. Barbara Rood was Waylon's third wife, and they were married at her parents' home on October 22, 1967 just as soon as his divorce with Lynne was final.

6 - NASHVILLE

You may remember Bobby Bare. He recorded a big pop single called "All-American Boy" which peaked at number two in 1958. He had just been drafted into the army and wasn't there to overlook the releasing of the record. It was released as being sung by Bill Parsons. However, people on the inside knew the difference. When he got out of the army, he started to look for work in music and started recording under his own name, Bobby Bare. By 1964, Bare had put three songs into the Top 10 on the Country charts.

It so happened that Bobby Bare and Don Bowman were friends and, since Bowman had worked with Waylon on several songs, he was always talking up Waylon whenever he had any contact with Bobby. Bobby largely ignored Waylon until one day in 1964. He was driving through Phoenix, on his way to Las Vegas, when a song came on the radio that had been recorded when Waylon was with A&M. However, the song was never released nationally and so Bobby hadn't heard it before. The song was "Just to Satisfy You." This would later become a big song for Waylon but, for now, Bobby Bare wanted to record it. He stopped in Phoenix, went to JD's to see Waylon and his band play, and decided he should have talked to Waylon a long time before this.

Bobby called his producer, Chet Atkins, who worked in Nashville for RCA Records, and told him he had to hear this guy. Turns out, Chet had heard of Waylon Jennings, but he had never heard his music. Two other performers had told Atkins that he should pay attention to Waylon. They were Skeeter Davis and Duane Eddy, both moderately popular. When Atkins heard "Just to Satisfy You" and another song, "Four Strong Winds," he wanted Waylon to come to Nashville and talk about a contract. Bobby Bare ended up recording "Four Strong Winds," which was a Top 10 song for him in late 1964 and then he covered "Just to Satisfy You" in mid-1965. It only reached 31 on the Country charts. Waylon did much better with the song.

This was the break Waylon was looking for. He now had a chance to record for RCA Records, a major label with people who knew what they were doing. He called Herb Alpert in California and asked to be let out of the contract with A&M. Alpert was not particularly attached to Waylon, and his records weren't selling anyway, so he said yes. Waylon was on his way to Nashville.

The entire band, along with Barbara Rood, went to Nashville with Waylon. It meant giving up a great gig in Phoenix that was earning them good money and taking a chance on National fame. The last night they played in JD's, there were two thousand people there to see them off. The floor was so packed that nobody could dance.

It was March of 1965 when Waylon and his caravan rolled into Nashville. He was driving a yellow Cadillac with Barbara on his arm, and the band was all crammed into a Chevy flower car, which is really a hearse. The three band members and all of their gear was in the car, and they drove all the way from Phoenix to Nashville. They started recording right away. They recorded twelve songs, one of which was Waylon's first record to chart on the Country charts. The song was "That's the Chance I'll Have to Take," and it hit number 49 on the charts. Not great, but a good first effort. RCA was happy and so they kept recording. The song was released on May 4th but didn't hit the charts until August 21st.

Most of the twelve songs that they recorded in that first session were slated to go on an album, *Folk-Country,* which wasn't released until March 14, 1966. That's a long time to wait, from March until August, for the single and even longer for the album to start getting some return for their work. There was no money coming in, so they travelled back to Phoenix and resumed their old life, hoping that fame was just around the corner.

Waylon made three trips to Nashville that year, cleaning up things he had recorded and recording new material to prepare for the album *Folk-Country*. The songs they were releasing were doing better and better on the charts. After that first release, "That's the Chance I'll Have to Take," his second release, "Stop the World (I Want to Get Off)," reached number sixteen. Next was "Anita, You're Dreaming" which peaked at number seventeen. This song was written about Barbara Rood. He wrote the song with Don Bowman when he first met Barbara and was still married to Lynne. He didn't see a future for him and Barbara and was trying to tell her she was dreaming if she thought they could be together. Dreams do come true, sometimes.

Folk-Country was released in March of 1966 and contained four songs that were written by Waylon. The other eight were written by friend Don Bowman and other Nashville writers. Chet Atkins let the three band members who made up The Waylors play on the album. This was unusual in that record companies often brought in an entirely different band to play on recordings than who the people saw at the live shows. This was especially true for new performers who the public did not know.

With the release of his album, which peaked at number nine on the Billboard Country Album Charts, Waylon felt it was time to move to Nashville and give up Phoenix altogether. He got a booking agent named W.E. "Lucky" Moeller. Lucky provided the band with work on the road while they waited for the money to start coming in from the sales of the records.

7 - JOHNNY CASH

Back when Waylon was in Lubbock, he met June Carter when she came through with her family. Through June, he met Johnny Cash, who was trying to get June to marry him. They eventually got married in 1968 but, for now, Johnny was between wives. The two hit it off right away. They became instant friends and stayed friends their entire lives. Johnny made the off-hand comment that when Waylon came to Nashville, the two of them should live together. So, now that Waylon was in Nashville, he went to find Cash.

The two of them found an apartment and lived together for several months. Waylon said the place was so small that there was hardly any room to turn around when they were both there. Fortunately, it was rare when they were both there. One or the other was always out on tour somewhere. You might wonder what happened to Barbara when Waylon moved in with Johnny. Waylon could not have her live with him because their relationship was supposed to be a secret. He was still married to Lynne and didn't want to do anything to rock that boat. Therefore, they kept it secret until the divorce actually came through in 1967. Barbara got a room in the same apartment house where Waylon and Johnny lived, so she wasn't far away. Johnny was single at the time. His marriage to June Carter hadn't happened yet, so he was fine with the arrangement.

One problem Waylon was having was that he was getting into drugs big time. He had taken amphetamines as far back as Salt Lake City. He had been taking them ever since, but the problem was getting bigger and bigger. Johnny Cash was also into drugs, and you can read about all of his adventures in *Legends of Country Music - Johnny Cash*. The two would bring their drugs home and hide them in the apartment. Both thought the other didn't know about their habits. Waylon says everyone in Nashville took drugs of one sort or another.

Everyone that is except Chet Atkins, and Chet didn't want his musicians taking drugs. Most of them would lie to him when he asked if they were using, but Waylon refused to do that and told him straight out that he was using. Chet was mad for a while but got over it. Waylon kept recording.

Waylon continued to work on his second album, *Leavin' Town,* which he recorded in February of 1966. However, it wasn't released until October. He was still singing country music that was sort-of middle-of-the-road. He hadn't gotten to the Seventies when he would become part of the Outlaw music that became popular then. *Leavin' Town* contained the song "Anita, You're Dreaming" which I've already talked about. The song peaked at number seventeen. The biggest hit from the album was a Gordon Lightfoot composed song called "(That's What You Get) For Lovin' Me." It was Waylon's first time in the Top 10 when it entered the charts on September 3, 1966 and peaked at number nine.

8 - NASHVILLE REBEL

Waylon's third album was *Nashville Rebel*, which I think describes him pretty well. It's actually the soundtrack of a movie by the same name which was shot in 1966 and released in October. The album reached number four on the Country Album chart. The soundtrack doesn't look like it contains anything but one Waylon song and a few instrumentals used as background music. There were a lot of songs done in the movie itself by other performers, like Loretta Lynn and Sonny James. These are not on the soundtrack album. The only song to chart from the album was "Green River" which reached number eleven, and it was written by Harlan Howard. The only song on the album in which Waylon did any of the writing was "Nashville Bum," which did not chart.

This was the first time Waylon had acted. He had never had any aspirations to be an actor and says he was just passing the auditions office when, on a whim, he walked in and read for the leading part. He says he was terrible and didn't give it another thought until they called him and told him he had the role. He suspects Chet Atkins had something to do with that.

The movie is a B-movie about a guy who had just gotten out of the army and is wandering the back roads of the south when he is mugged and his money stolen. He's beaten up but makes his way to a town where he finds the female lead of the movie, Mary Frann. She nurses him back to health, and the two fall in love and are married. He has a guitar and sings in the movie and eventually becomes a star. One reviewer on imdb.com calls it *Jail House Rock* with Waylon instead of Elvis. The only place I could find the movie to watch it (without paying Amazon $20 for the DVD) was on YouTube. It's a typical Sixties movie and didn't make much money, but it's enjoyable to watch. I enjoyed seeing some of the stars of country music when they were young. Some stars in the movie are gone now, and that makes it extra special.

The film is full of performers from that era, people like Porter Wagoner, Chet Atkins, Sonny James, Loretta Lynn, and Tex Ritter. Mary Frann, who played Waylon's love interest in the film, went on to many more roles on television, perhaps the most famous of which was as Bob Newhart's wife in the sitcom, *Newhart*.

Waylon had to kiss Mary Frann in the movie, and Waylon says this just drove Barbara crazy. They'd been married less than a year, and Barbara was suspicious of everything Waylon did. He says all of his first three wives were like that. It seemed like music and performing were the "other woman." Barbara and Waylon argued all the time. If he was home (which was rare), they argued in person. If he was away on the road, they argued over the phone. She wanted him to give up the music business, but he wasn't willing to do that.

In all honesty, Waylon was doing exactly what Barbara suspected he was doing. He would get with every girl he could while he was on the road. In a twist of irony, Barbara hired a female private detective to watch Waylon and report on him, and she ended up in his bed. I guess she had her evidence.

The girls increased, and the drugs increased. Waylon was on the road to self-destruction. He took twenty to thirty amphetamines a day. He took them to sleep and then took them to wake up. He says he never had a hangover because he never stopped taking pills and drinking long enough to get one. On June 3, 1968, Waylon's father passed away. Waylon was shook up and refused to go to the viewing. He came to the funeral, however, but during it, he passed out.

Waylon made his first appearance on the *Grand Ole Opry* on January 27, 1967. He desperately wanted to be a part of the Opry and would one day, but when they asked him if he would come every Saturday night and sing a song, he turned them down. Saturday was the night of the week when he needed to be playing in the clubs and bars as the band toured the country. He didn't have the money or the time to go back to Nashville every week to play the Opry. He was very disappointed that he couldn't.

Life with Barbara had become harder and harder until, sometime in 1968, she left, and they were divorced. Waylon says that he took her home for the last time just a couple weeks after his father died. That would put their separation about July 1, 1968. Try as I might, I cannot find an exact date for the divorce. Waylon was on the road constantly. He managed to get back to Nashville now and then to record a record, but the concerts on the road took up most of his time. He said that the road trips were not really about the music. They were about the partying. He was high and/or drunk most of the time. He would pass out in hotels and wake up later not knowing what day it was or where he was.

9 - EARLY RECORDS

During 1967, Waylon recorded three albums, none of which produced a significant single, but all of which hit the album charts on Billboard, although with varying degrees of success. First there was *Waylon Sings Ol' Harlan,* which only peaked at number 32, but that was OK because to Waylon, it was a labour of love. Waylon and Harlan Howard were good friends by this time, and Harlan had written several songs which Waylon had recorded. Now, Waylon could honour his friend with an entire album of just Harlan Howard songs.

Next in 1967 came *Love of the Common People* which was released in August of 1967. It did much better on the charts, peaking at number three. Waylon says he likes the title song because it's the story of a country boy who follows his dream and eventually becomes a big country singer. It's basically Waylon's story. Even more important, *Love of the Common People* is when we can see that Waylon is developing his own sound. Chet Atkins wanted everyone in Nashville to sound like the "Nashville Sound," and Waylon hated that. He wanted to sound like himself and develop his own style, and this album allowed him to do that.

The last album of 1967 was *The One and Only* which was released in November. This album peaked at number 19 on the Billboard Country Album Charts. It only has two songs which were co-written by Waylon. The rest of the album are covers. He gives a nod to Roy Orbison with the song "Dream Baby." Back in Phoenix when he played at JD's, his imitation of Roy Orbison was well-known. He could sing exactly like him.

Waylon was making himself known more and more as 1967 turned into 1968 and 1968 turned into 1969. "The Chokin' Kind" was his biggest hit of 1967. Recorded in Nashville on April 27, 1967, it was, like many others, written by Harlan Howard. It entered the Billboard Country Charts on August 19, 1967 and peaked at number eight, which was Waylon's highest ranking song until this time. It was the only hit to come from Waylon's fifth album, *Hangin' On*, which was released in February of 1968. Soul singer Joe Simon covered this song in 1969, peaking at number thirteen on the pop charts and number one on the Hot Black Singles chart.

His next three hits would put him higher and higher on the charts. First is a haunting ballad about losing a girl but being unable to forget her. "Walk On Out of My Mind," which was written by Red Lane, was from the album *Only the Greatest* and hit number five on the singles charts in January of 1968. *Only the Greatest* sounds like a Greatest Hits album but it wasn't. It did contain two top 10 songs: the aforementioned "Walk On Out of My Mind" and a song which should be familiar to every Waylon Jennings fan, "Only Daddy That'll Walk the Line." "Daddy" was written by Ivy J. Bryant II, also known as Jimmy Bryant, and just missed being Waylon's first number one song, peaking at number two in July of 1968. This song became a staple of Waylon's shows. He almost always sang it when he was performing. "Daddy" was kept out of the top spot by "Mama Tried" by Merle Haggard and then Jeanie C. Riley hopped right over him with "Harper Valley PTA." He spent five weeks at number two. Probably a little bit disappointing, but it was his biggest hit to date, so he had to feel good about that.

Between the two songs from the *Only the Greatest* album, he put another song in the Top 10. "I Got You" was the first time Waylon had sung a duet (at least in a charted song). He sang this song with Anita Carter who was from the famous Carter family that Johnny Cash married into. She was the daughter of Ezra and Maybelle Carter and the sister of June Carter Cash. The song reached number four on the singles charts. Don't confuse this song with "I Got You, Babe" which was a number one single on the pop charts in 1965 by Sonny and Cher.

The two are totally different songs. "I Got You" was the only hit from the album *Just to Satisfy You*. Now everyone knows that "Just to Satisfy You" was a big hit for Waylon but not the version recorded on this album. He wouldn't hit the charts with "Just to Satisfy You" until 1982 when he had another duet, this time with Willie Nelson. Stay tuned.

Chet Atkins decided he was tired of producing and wanted to get back to playing music, so he gave Waylon over to Danny Davis and went back to playing the guitar. The only problem was Danny and Waylon just did not get along. Waylon says they were like oil and water. Danny Davis was the leader of a group of musicians called The Nashville Brass. They had more of an orchestral sound to their music than traditional country. They had lots of brass instruments, as you can imagine. The Nashville Brass didn't have many hits. "Night Life" peaked at number twenty in 1980, and that was as high as they got. The success of that song is probably because Willie Nelson was singing along with them. The main thing The Nashville Brass accomplished was that they started moving country from a more traditional sound toward a more pop sound, and Waylon didn't like that.

The song "MacArthur Park" was written by the great Jimmy Webb and first recorded by the actor Richard Harris. It was a number two hit on the pop charts in the spring of 1968. Waylon heard the song and decided he would like to record it. He had met a group called the Kimberlys in Las Vegas and was somewhat involved with Verna Kimberly, one of the lead singers. He went back to RCA and convinced them to record an album with the Kimberlys. That album was *Country Folk* and was released in August of 1969. The lead song on the album was the combined efforts of Waylon and the Kimberlys doing "MacArthur Park." If you listen to the song, it doesn't sound that country. The strings and arrangement make it almost sound like a pop song. That is the influence of Danny Davis. Waylon was happy with the result, although he would have liked some changes to it. The song reached number 23 on the charts and then it won a Grammy for *Best Country Performance by a Duo or Group* on March 11, 1970. Years later, Waylon had the occasion to meet Richard Harris. Harris grabbed Waylon in a friendly way and said, "You're the one who stole my Grammy."

We end the Sixties with an album which is Waylon's first "Greatest Hits" album. It is called *The Best of Waylon Jennings* and wasn't released until June of 1970, but the two singles that were chart hits both hit the charts in 1969. The album contains mostly songs that have appeared on other Waylon Jennings' albums over the last few years. The first was "Something's Wrong in California," which peaked at number nineteen. The song was written by Wayne Carson and Rodney Lay. It's a nice ballad, but there's not much online as to the origin of the song. I suspect this was just one of many that Waylon recorded to fill out the album. The second single from *The Best of Waylon Jennings* was "The Days of Sand and Shovels" which peaked at number twenty. It was written by Doyle Marsh and George Reneau and, like the other song, that's about all we know. They are pleasant to listen to, however.

The next single was an interesting record because it is a classic of rock and roll. The song, "Brown Eyed Handsome Man," was originally recorded and written by Chuck Berry back in 1956. It was later covered by Buddy Holly, which I'm sure is why Waylon recorded it. In January of 1970, he recorded his tenth album for RCA, simply called *Waylon*. The album reached number fourteen on the country album chart and had just one hit, "Brown Eyed Handsome Man." The single was his fifth Top 5 song, hitting the singles charts on November 22, 1969 and peaking at number three.

10 - ON THE ROAD

With as many Top 10 songs under Waylon's belt, and with as many albums as he had recorded, you would think he was sitting pretty money-wise. But that wasn't true; not yet, at least. The band was on the road three hundred days a year, and they still weren't making any money. One reason they were broke was because of the drugs that were passing through the group every day. Waylon once spent nine days and nights living on pills and gambling. He came close to dying several times.

On February 9, 1969, they were on an icy road on their way to play in Peoria, Illinois. They were driving an old camper with a compartment over the truck cab. His bass player, Chuck Conway, was asleep in that compartment. Conway had only joined the group a couple weeks earlier. As they tried to cross a river on the Kickapoo Creek Bridge, the truck slid on the icy road and sheared off the compartment, and Conway went into the river. Conway was killed instantly. Waylon, fortunately, wasn't with them. He was driving his own car about thirty minutes behind them and when he arrived on the scene, the place was crawling with police. One cop had found drugs on the truck, but told Waylon, "You've got enough troubles" and threw the drugs away.

Waylon was devastated. He had not known Conway well, since he had just joined the band, but he felt somehow responsible for his death. In reality, there was nothing he could have done to prevent this. I have to think Waylon remembered back almost exactly ten years earlier to February of 1959 when we lost Buddy Holly and the others.

Life went on. They got a new bass player and continued touring. In Canada, some of the band members got into a big fight and were arrested for possession. Waylon got them out of jail and when they returned home, heading for Nashville, they were stopped at the

Canadian border, searched, and arrested again for possessing marijuana. Once more, they went to jail, and Waylon had to bail them out. Richie Albright, his drummer, had had enough. He knew he needed to clean himself up and left the band for a short time. The date was October 25, 1969. The next day, on October 26, 1969, Waylon married Jessi Colter.

11 - JESSI COLTER

Jessi Colter was born Mirriam Johnson on May 25, 1943 in Phoenix, Arizona. She grew up in a Pentecostal home, her mother being a preacher for the church and her father a race-car driver. Sounds like an interesting household. She learned the piano when she was young and began playing in church when she was eleven. She graduated from Mesa High School in 1961 and decided she wanted to sing for a living. She had a lot of trouble getting started. She took jobs singing in local clubs in Phoenix, and it was in one of these that she met Duane Eddy.

You might remember Duane Eddy. He was a guitar player in the late Fifties and early Sixties who had fifteen hits on the Top 40 pop charts. The two biggest of these were "Rebel Rouser," which hit number six in 1958, and "Because They're Young," which made it to number four in 1960. Eddy had a great career and, in the early Sixties, he was living in Phoenix. He met Mirriam, and the two were married in 1961. After the marriage, Mirriam recorded two records, the first being "Lonesome Road." It got some play but not enough to make the charts. Her second single did nothing at all, and she "retired" from recording for several years.

She first met Waylon in 1966 when Duane brought her by the studio where Waylon was recording. She was a married woman (which rarely stopped Waylon), but this time he didn't make a move on her. After all, Duane Eddy was right there. Waylon says he felt a spark when he first saw her, and it seemed she felt the same way, but neither of them acted on it at that first meeting. In 1968, Mirriam divorced Duane Eddy and the next time they met, Waylon knew this was something he wanted. By now, she had changed her name to Jessi Colter. She named herself after her great-grandmother, Jesse Colter, the spelling is just a little different. Jessi was a pistol. She never took lip from anyone, and she spoke her mind. That upset Waylon a little in the beginning, but he soon got used to it and actually enjoyed it. They were married on October 26, 1969 in Mesa, Arizona. He got it right this time. They were still together when he died in 2002.

By October 29th, they were back in Nashville where he recorded "Singer of Sad Songs." It was the title song of the album *Singer of Sad Songs,* which came out over a year later in November of 1970. The single reached number twelve on the charts whereas the album only got to number twenty-three. That was the only single from the album which reached the charts, and it was the only song recorded in Nashville. The rest of the album was recorded in Hollywood with producer Lee Hazelwood. This really upset Waylon. He was ready to leave RCA and try his luck somewhere else, but he didn't. He didn't like the fact that RCA seemed to think Nashville wasn't necessary and that everything should be recorded on the West Coast or the East Coast. Waylon said that if you were a country artist out of Nashville, they treated you like you were an uninvited guest. Nashville was country, and that was where it should stay.

His next album was called *The Taker/Tulsa*, recorded during the last part of 1969 and the first part of 1970. It did a little better than the previous album. It reached number twelve on the album chart and spawned three singles which hit the Top 40. The first was the title song, "The Taker," which did very well, peaking at number five. "The Taker" was written by a new writer, Kris Kristofferson, who was just beginning to make his mark in the music world, and Shel Silverstein. Kristofferson wrote four of the songs on the album. The greatest of these, at least for me, is "Lovin' Her Was Easier (Than Anything I'll Ever Do Again)." This did not chart for Waylon, but The Glaser Brothers covered it in 1981, and it was a number two hit for them. I've also heard Kris sing it. While it wasn't a hit for him, (he did not make the country charts but had his first crossover to the pop charts where it peaked at number 26 in 1971), he does a great job on the song.

The other two singles from *The Taker/Tulsa* were "(Don't Let the Sun Set on You) Tulsa" (recorded on October 29, 1969) which peaked at number sixteen in December of 1969 and "Mississippi Woman" (not recorded until three months later in February of 1970) which peaked at number fourteen in April. In between these three singles from *The Taker/Tulsa*, Waylon got together with his new wife, and the two of them recorded a live single called "Suspicious Minds" which, as you might guess, is a cover of the Elvis Presley song. The song was released as a single in 1970 but only got as far as number 23 on the charts. I cannot find any album it was a part of until 1976 when it was included on *Wanted! The Outlaws*, an album which went to number one on the country charts and number ten on the pop charts. We'll discuss more about *Wanted!* later.

12 - THE BEGINNINGS OF OUTLAW

It would be an understatement to say that Waylon was not happy with RCA. They were a record assembly line and just wanted to put out music that sounded like every other piece of music that was being released. RCA was headquartered in New York and really didn't understand the country genre. They wanted Waylon to sound more modern, less traditional. This "Nashville Sound" had been around since the mid-Fifties, and several country performers had adopted it, like Jim Reeves and Ferlin Husky, but Waylon wanted to sound different. He was constantly fighting with them to play his own sound. Chet Atkins was asked at one point what exactly the Nashville Sound was. He reached into his pocket and rattled his change. "That's what it is," he said. "The sound of money."

Luckily, Waylon wasn't alone in his dislike of the Nashville Sound. Others wanted an edgier sound to country, people like Willie Nelson and Kris Kristofferson. Waylon got a new producer, Ronnie Light, who was new and reluctant to say no to his artists, and Waylon could record the album he really wanted to record. The album was called *Good Hearted Woman* and was recorded over a two-year period, from 1969 to 1971. It was released in February of 1972. The album rose to number seven on the Billboard albums chart. The title song "Good Hearted Woman" was recorded in September of 1970 and released on December 14th. It peaked at number three on the singles chart and became an instant classic.

There are various stories as to the origin of this song, but this is what I believe. The song was written by Waylon and Willie Nelson. They were staying together in a hotel in Fort Worth, Texas when Waylon saw an ad in the newspaper promoting Tina Turner, who was in town on tour. The ad said Turner was "a good-hearted woman loving two-timing men," the latter part referring to her husband, Ike Turner. Tina and Ike were still together but would split up in 1976 and divorce by 1979. Waylon thought those words would make a good song, so he hunted down Willie who was in a poker game somewhere in the hotel, and the two of them worked on the lyrics and melody for the song while the game was going on. Consequently, writing credit is given to both Waylon and Willie for writing the song.

The second song from the *Good Hearted Woman* album was "Sweet Dream Woman." The song was written by Chip Taylor and Al Gorgoni, both well-known songwriters, and the song peaked at number seven on the singles charts. The album *Good Hearted Woman* was the beginning of what was later called the Outlaw Era. The term hadn't been coined yet, but it was coming.

The term "Outlaw" originated with a lady named Hazel Smith. She was a Nashville media specialist and worked primarily for Hillbilly Central. One day, she was asked by a disc jockey working for WCSE-FM in Asheboro, North Carolina what to call this new music coming out of Nashville. Hazel said it was called Outlaw Music, and the name stuck. Waylon says Outlaw is more an attitude than a type of music. It means standing up for your rights, your own way of doing things. Waylon says the greatest Outlaw of all time is Hank Williams, and the term hadn't even been invented yet when he was alive.

Richie Albright, Waylon's former drummer, came back to the band in early 1972. Richie had been gone since 1969 and had spent that time cleaning himself up. Waylon says that when he left, he went back to Phoenix, locked himself in a room, and just ate, slept, and smoked pot. Oddly enough, smoking pot was the way he got off the pills he had been taking.

Richie was shocked when he saw Waylon. Waylon had hepatitis, was in the hospital, and had deteriorated into a depressed, constantly on drugs, pathetic human being ready to quit the recording business and return to Phoenix where he knew he was loved. Things had gotten terrible. Richie told Waylon he should give it one more try. Richie had someone he wanted Waylon to meet. His name was Neil Reshen, and he was not a lawyer, he was not an accountant and, most importantly, he was not southern. But he could negotiate. He was one of the best in the country, and Richie introduced Waylon to him. Reshen had worked with some big names in rock. He was a business manager at *Creem* magazine and had run the careers of the jazz great Miles Davis and the iconic Frank Zappa. Reshen soon became Waylon's manager and later would also become Willie Nelson's manager. When Waylon negotiated his next contract with RCA, Reshen was there and told Waylon, "Don't say a word. The one who speaks first loses."

RCA ended up giving Waylon the best contract he had ever had. The next thing Waylon did was fire his manager Lucky Moeller and hire Neil Reshen. There were still problems with royalties, however. Sometimes, Waylon would have a bestseller and seemed to get no money at all. Reshen stepped in and helped him with that. RCA knew that Waylon was on the threshold of a big hit and didn't want to lose him. They were right.

On July 4th, 1973, Waylon took part in the first of the famous Willie Nelson *Fourth of July Picnic,* held in Dripping Springs, Texas. This is a tradition that Willie had carried on for years, and it has just gotten bigger and bigger. Sort of like a Woodstock for country fans. This year (2019), it's being held in the Auston360 Amphitheater in Del Valle, a suburb of Austin, Texas.

13 - "THIS TIME"

One perk of the new contract was that Waylon was now free to record wherever he wanted. In addition, he could create his own label. Consequently, that is what he did. He moved his recording to a location he could control and, most importantly, could take his band with him. Now it was his live band we heard on the records, not the studio band that RCA insisted they use. This saved a lot of money. The label he created was WGJ Productions, which stood for "Waylon Goddamn Jennings." Not much would come from having that label. Being a production company, the logo appeared on very few records. Almost everything Waylon released for the next ten years came out on the RCA label.

After *Good Hearted Woman,* Waylon recorded *Ladies Love Outlaws,* which peaked at number eleven on the album charts but did not produce any singles. This was later considered to be number two in a "trilogy" of Outlaw albums that Waylon recorded in the early Seventies, before the name became popular. The third album of the trilogy was *Lonesome On'ry and Mean.* This third album produced two singles, both of which made the Top 10 on the country charts. It was the first album Waylon produced himself (with a little help from Ronny Light). The first charting single was "Pretend I Never Happened" which was written by Willie Nelson and reached number six. The second charting single was "You Can Have Her," written by William S. Cook and which peaked at number seven.

He next recorded an album which continued the Outlaw subgenre. *Honky Tonk Heroes* was recorded in early 1973 and released in July. Waylon had met a songwriter named Billy Joe Shaver and had committed to recording some of his songs. Shaver wanted to be a country singer except that he had lost two of the fingers on one hand during an accident. He taught himself to play the guitar without the fingers but never really broke out as a singer. Instead, he wrote country music. Waylon was impressed enough with him that every song but one on the *Honky Tonk Heroes* albums is written by Shaver. Shaver had a long career in Nashville as a writer and even recorded a couple albums, but they didn't do much. The one Top 10 song on the album was "You Ask Me Too" which peaked at number eight.

Critics initially panned the album *Honky Tonk Heroes*. It was different from what was being played in Nashville. Soon, however, the public started getting it, and it ended up peaking at number fourteen on the country album charts. The album has become one of the most important albums in the history of country music. The album is listed in the book *1001 Albums You Must Hear Before You Die*, by Robert Dimery.

Now that Waylon had more control over his recording, he resurrected a song he had written four years earlier. It was called "This Time" and, at the time, RCA said it wasn't any good and wouldn't let him record it. Now that he was, more or less, on his own, he decided to record and release it, with Willie Nelson producing.

Waylon had moved into a new recording studio, called "Hillbilly Central," owned by Tompall Glaser, so he wouldn't be bothered by RCA executives. There, he recorded his next album also called *This Time*. The album peaked at number four on the album charts. More importantly, Waylon had his first number one single with the title song "This Time." The song entered the Top 40 on April 27, 1974 and hit number one on June 22. This was his first number one. There would be fifteen more (including duets and his time with The Highwaymen). One thing to note about the album, *This Time,* besides containing his first number one single, this was also the first time he had recorded a song written by his wife Jessi Colter. The song was called "Mona" and writing credit was given to Mirriam Eddy, Jessi's name before she married Waylon. The song did not chart.

14 - Dreaming My Dreams With You

Waylon and Willie Nelson had been friends for years. Waylon attended his "picnics" on the Fourth of July at Willie's ranch when he could, and they spoke the same language. Willie had gotten sick of the bureaucracy in Nashville long before Waylon did. In 1972, Willie had left Nashville to go back to Texas where he worked regularly. He wasn't making much money, but it had never been about the money; it was always about the music. Willie had worked for RCA but, like Waylon, was sick of the constant criticism of his work, so he quit the label. Soon, he was recording for Atlantic Records, who had just opened a new country division.

RCA did not want Waylon to follow that same path and so they eased up on the bureaucracy and let him have more control over his recording. Waylon was happy about that and soon was putting out records that sounded nothing like the rest of what Nashville releasing. His next single was "I'm a Ramblin' Man" written by Ray Pennington back in 1967. Pennington had recorded the song himself and took it to number 29. Waylon thought he could do better than that, so he recorded the song as part of his next album, *The Ramblin' Man,* and had his second number one single on the country charts on August 10, 1974. The album peaked at number three and tied his former record for any album he had recorded so far. He hadn't hit number three with an album since 1967. *The Ramblin' Man* was not as outlaw as had been his earlier albums.

The second song from *The Ramblin' Man* to hit the Top 10 was "Rainy Day Women." Written by Waylon, it was released on December 21, 1974 and peaked at number two on the singles charts.

Dreaming My Dreams With You was Waylon's twenty-second album. It was released in June of 1975 and, on September 6th, made it all the way to number one on the country album charts. It was recorded in Glaser's Hillbilly Central in Nashville. Waylon co-produced the album as he took more and more control for his recordings. The album had two charting singles, the first of which is the title song "Dreaming My Dreams With You," which peaked at number ten. Allen Reynolds, who has written many country songs, wrote the song. "Dreaming My Dreams With You" was covered by at least fifteen other artists, including Emmylou Harris and Alison Krauss. Waylon says in his autobiography that *Dreaming My Dreams With You* was his favorite album of all the ones he recorded.

The second of the songs from *Dreaming My Dreams With You* was "Are You Sure Hank Done It This Way" which was not only a number one song but became one of Waylon's signature songs. The song hit number one on November 15, 1975. It spent just one week there, but it was enough to make this one of the all-time classic country songs. The song is really a tribute to the old style country that RCA and Nashville were trying to replace with a more modern sound. Waylon sang it in almost every concert he did after this. The B-side of "Hank" was "Bob Wills is Still the King," which did not chart except as a B-side but continued the notion that country ought to remain traditional. Waylon would lose that fight.

On October 13, 1975, the *Country Music Association Awards* (CMA) were handed out at the Grand Ole Opry in Nashville. Waylon had been nominated for *Entertainer of the Year* and for *Male Vocalist of the Year*. Waylon had been nominated for *Male Vocalist of the Year* in 1974 but lost to Ronnie Milsap. The next year, in 1975, he won *Male Vocalist of the Year,* and this was his first award from the CMA. He did not get *Entertainer of the Year*, however; that went to John Denver. The broadcast of the show resulted in one of the more memorable moments in television history (at least for Country Music).

Charlie Rich had won *Entertainer of the Year* in 1974 and so got the opportunity to announce to the crowd who the new *Entertainer of the Year* was. He opened the envelope, just stood there looking at it for a few seconds, said the name "John Denver," then took out his lighter, and set fire to the card. Later Rich said it was just a joke, but the CMA thought it was serious enough to ban him for several years from the CMA Awards. Many think it was a protest against the direction country music was headed, but Rich says he didn't intend that.

In early 1975, Jessi Colter had her first solo hit with "I'm Not Lisa." It's a song about a man who accidentally calls his wife by another name. She had hit the country Top 40 twice before but as duets with Waylon. Now, she had her own hit, and it went to number one on the country charts and to number four on the pop charts. Jessi was suddenly her own person, not living in the shadow of Waylon anymore. Jessi would have thirteen Top 40 hits in country, but she never hit number one again. "I'm Not Lisa" was the only song that crossed over to the pop charts.

15 - WANTED! THE OUTLAWS

RCA was suddenly on-board with the Outlaw movement. Giving it a name was a big step forward since they could market it as something special. Waylon was selling records, and they couldn't deny that. Therefore, they encouraged him to record more Outlaw. The album that resulted from that discussion was *Wanted! The Outlaws*. The album was released on January 12, 1976 and re-issued almost exactly twenty years later on February 15, 1996. In 1976, the album went to number one on the country album chart on February 28th and stayed there for six weeks. It also peaked at number ten on the pop album charts. The interesting thing about *Wanted! The Outlaws* was that there was practically no new music on the album. It was mainly made up of earlier material which had been tweaked a little. The only new song was "My Heroes Have Always Been Cowboys."

One example of a hit from the past was "Good Hearted Woman." The first time Waylon recorded it as a solo effort back in 1971, it got to number three. This time, Willie Nelson joined him, and it became a number one hit on the country single charts. It also became Waylon's first crossover hit when it peaked at number 25 on the pop charts. The artist names given on the single is just "Waylon and Willie." Everybody knew their last names. The song appears to be a live version. Some say that the song was recorded at Geno McCoslin's Western Place in Dallas, Texas. However, in Waylon's autobiography, he says that the "live" portions were inserted electronically to give the appearance of being live. I will let you decide.

At the 1976 *Country Music Association Awards* (CMA's), "Good Hearted Woman" won *Single of the Year* and the album *Wanted! The Outlaws* won *Album of the Year*. *Wanted! The Outlaws* was the first country album in the history of the charts to be certified platinum, selling over a million copies. I especially like the cover of the album. This was not just a Waylon Jennings album; it was a collaboration between Waylon, Willie, Jessi, and Tompall Glaser. The cover looks like an old wanted poster with pictures of the four of them.

The second (and last) single from the album was "Suspicious Minds" recorded by Waylon and Jessi back in 1971. Waylon updated the arrangement a little, and this time it peaked at number two.

One other song should be mentioned from *Wanted! The Outlaws.* "My Heroes Have Always Been Cowboys" was the lead song on side one of the album. This was recorded by Waylon but never charted as a single. Willie, however, picked up the song in 1980 and sang his own version which appears on the soundtrack of the movie *The Electric Horseman* starring Robert Redford. Willie's version of the song peaked at number one on the country charts and stayed there for two weeks.

By the mid-Seventies, Waylon was putting out about an album a year. IIis 1975 album had been *Dreaming My Dreams* and, in 1976, he released *Are You Ready for the Country*. I'm not counting the *Wanted!* Album as that was a collaboration and not a solo album.

Are You Ready for the Country was his second number one album in a row (third if you count *Wanted!*). Recorded during several months in early 1976, it was released in June and hit number one August 14th. It would eventually spend ten weeks at the top of the album charts. It had an initial two-week run in August, left the number one spot for a week, and then returned on September 4th for a four-week run. It then fell out of the top spot for two weeks and then returned for one week on October 16th. It fell out again for eight weeks, returning on December 18th for a final three-week run. That's a total of ten weeks spread over five months. Waylon was truly on top of the country world.

There were two singles from the *Are You Ready for the Country* album. The first was "Can't You See." The song was written by Toy Caldwell, then a member of the Marshall Tucker Band. The Marshall Tucker Band, known for that southern rock sound, had some success on the country charts but very little on the pop charts. They released "Can't You See" as their first single, but it did not chart on either charts. Waylon recorded it in 1976, and it peaked at number four on the country charts.

The second single from the *Are You Ready for the Country* album was the title song, "Are You Ready For the Country." The great Neil Young wrote the song. He recorded it in 1973, with his buddies Graham Nash and David Crosby singing backup. People to this day have debated if Neil Young was planning on a switch to country music or if he was talking about something else altogether. The song is considered country rock. When Waylon recorded the song, he changed a couple lines in the lyrics. Where Neil sings, "Are you ready for the country/Because it's time to go," Waylon changed it to, "Are you ready for the country/Are you ready for me?" If you look for the video on YouTube, try to find the interview on Ralph Emery's show. Neil and Waylon sing the song together at about the six minute mark in the video. It's great to hear the duet, and they use Waylon's lyrics, not Neil's, which I thought was very cool.

Waylon's version of "Are You Ready for the Country" peaked at number seven on the country single charts. That's a shame because I think it's a much better song than that.

Other songs on the *Are You Ready for the Country* album included "MacArthur Park (revisited)" which was an updated version of the 1969 hit. Also, there is a song written by Waylon called "Old Friend," a tribute to his old friend, Buddy Holly.

1976 would end with another annual *Country Music Association Awards*, on October 11th. They nominated Waylon for six awards, and he won three of them: *Album of the Year* for *Wanted! The Outlaws*, *Single of the Year* which he shared with Willie Nelson for "Good Hearted Woman," and *Vocal Duo of the Year* which he also shared with Willie for the same song. If there had been any question as to Waylon's status in Nashville, there wasn't now, Waylon was now on top.

16 - COCAINE

By 1977, Waylon was up to a $1500/day cocaine habit. He excuses the habit by saying that everyone was doing it (which was probably true) and that the pressures of touring and performing constantly were enough to drive anyone to drugs (also probably true). The effect the coke had on him was to make his mind race very fast. He would have a thought about lyrics for a song and by the time he could pick up his pen to write it down, his mind had gone on to something else. It made it very difficult to write songs.

On August 24, 1977, his luck ran out. He was in the studio recording tracks for an album when one girl working there brought him a package that had just been delivered. He opened it just enough to discover that it contained cakes of cocaine. He left it there on the music stand for a few minutes when he heard some commotion from outside the studio. He heard someone say that they were from the DEA and that they were there to arrest Waylon for possession and intent to distribute. Waylon quickly hid the drugs and when the feds came into the studio, they wanted to know where the drugs were. Waylon played innocent and asked them if they had a warrant. They did but not for the studio itself, which was where the drugs were hidden. While Waylon was distracting them, Richie Albright, Waylon's drummer, got rid of the drugs by flushing them down the toilet. Now, there was no evidence. They arrested him anyway.

The famous attorney, Jay Goldberg, defended Waylon at his trial. If found guilty, he was facing fifteen years in federal prison. Goldberg had worked for many celebrities like Bono, Mick Jagger, and Willie Nelson. He had handled Donald Trump's first couple of divorces. He was a high-powered attorney. Without evidence, they couldn't convict him so soon the trial was over, and they let him go. Waylon says the whole thing cost him about $100,000. Using his life as an example, he wrote "Don't You Think This Outlaw Bit's Done Got Out of Hand" which was released as a single in 1978 and reached number five on the singles charts. Jay Goldberg told him, "This is as good as a confession," but Waylon didn't care. He released the song anyway and went on with his life. Of course, he did not stop using drugs. At least, not in 1977.

The next year, on April 24, 1978, Waylon's manager Mark Rothbaum, Neil Reshem's assistant, pleaded guilty to distributing cocaine and served jail time. Reshem was Willie Nelson's manager also, and Willie was so impressed by Rothbaum that he fired Reshem and hired Rothbaum (when he got out) to be his full-time manager.

In late 1976 (December), Waylon released his first live album, appropriately called *Waylon Live*. It went straight to number one on the country album charts and stayed there for six weeks. The album was taken from two main events which had occurred over two years earlier. He had recorded three shows with his band, The Waylors: one in *Dallas' Western Place* on September 25, 1974 and two more shows at the *Austin Texas Opry House* on September 26th and 27th. The finished album was comprised of eleven songs and represented Waylon and his band. There were even three songs on the album that had never appeared on any other album. The first was "T for Texas" by Jimmie Rodgers. The song had appeared on the *Wanted!* album, but Tompall Glaser sang it. The second was a Willie Nelson song "Me and Paul" (Waylon changed the words to "Me and Tompall" when he sang it live), and the third was called "The Last Letter," written by Rex Griffin.

There were so many live recordings that Waylon wanted to release a double album but, in 1974, no one was doing that in country music. However, in 1999, they released a revised CD which had the nine extra tracks that Waylon had wanted to include in the first version. Then, in 2003, they released another version of the album which contained 42 tracks taken from those three live shows. Now, the album is considered one of the greatest live albums ever released. It is essential to Waylon Jennings' fans.

17 - "LUCKENBACH, TEXAS (BACK TO THE BASICS OF LOVE)"

This song deserves its own chapter because the album it came from, *Ol' Waylon,* was Waylon's biggest album of his career, and "Luckenbach, Texas" was the biggest single of his career. Let's look at the album first. *Ol' Waylon* was released in April of 1977 and became his fifth number one album in a row, if you count *Wanted! The Outlaws* and *Waylon Live.* It stayed at number one for an astounding thirteen weeks. That means Waylon held the number one album spot for nineteen weeks during 1977.

Waylon had been producing his own albums for a few years now but felt like he might do better if he brought in a professional. He asked Chips Moman to produce *Ol' Waylon,* and he agreed. Moman was a big name producer who had worked with the likes of Elvis Presley and Tammy Wynette. He was also a Grammy Award-winning songwriter. He had written a song called "Luckenbach, Texas" with a friend of his, Bobby Emmons. The two presented the song to Waylon to include on *Ol' Waylon* because, he said, it has Waylon's name in it. At first, Waylon didn't like it. He said it sounded too much like another song called "Goodtime Charlie's Got the Blues" which was written by Danny O'Keefe and reached number nine on the pop charts. Even though Waylon didn't like the song (and never did), he recognized a hit when he heard it and agreed to record it. I think it's safe to say he was glad he did.

Neither Waylon nor Chips Moman had ever been to Luckenbach, Texas. It's just about the smallest town you will ever see. Maybe it's grown a little, but the latest census I can find shows it has a population of three. Yes, that's 3. Who cares what the town is really like; it's a great song and was a number one for Waylon. It entered the country charts on April 16, 1977 and spent six weeks at the top.

The song is about a couple who are too well off for their own good. Waylon sings that they live in this high society and that has put a strain on their marriage. They needed to get back to the basics of love, so let's go to Luckenbach, Texas with Waylon and Willie and the boys. We can listen to Hank Williams and Mickey Newbury's train songs. Mickey Newbury was a Nashville songwriter who wrote country songs between 1968 and 2003. "Blue Eyes Crying in the Rain" was written by Fred Rose and, most recently (in 1977), had been done by Willie Nelson. Willie steps in at the end of "Luckenbach, Texas" and sings the last verse. He switches the order of "Waylon and Willie" to "Willie and Waylon" and instead of referring to Newbury's train songs, he refers to Jerry Jeff's train songs. Jerry Jeff is Jerry Jeff Walker, who also is a country music songwriter and performer who is known for the song "Mr Bojangles."

One last piece of trivia about "Luckenbach, Texas" is that, believe it or not, Alvin and the Chipmunks covered the song in 1981 for their album *Urban Chipmunk*.

There were no other singles from *Ol' Waylon*, but it didn't need any. Just "Luckenbach, Texas" alone was able to make it the bestselling album of Waylon's career. Two other tracks deserve to be mentioned, however. He covered Kenny Rogers' very first solo hit "Lucille," but it was not released as a single. He also covered Neil Diamond's "Sweet Caroline." Waylon was a big fan of Diamond and has done his songs on other albums. He also recorded a song called "If You See Me Getting Smaller" by Jimmy Webb, a great songwriter. The song was interpreted in two different ways. One was that it was Waylon's way of acknowledging Willie Nelson's success, as he was gradually getting bigger than Waylon in his career. The other interpretation was that Waylon was talking about his gradual descent into drugs, as his habit had gotten worse and worse.

In the summer of 1977, Waylon and Willie petitioned the CMA to have their names removed from consideration for the 1977 *Country Music Association Awards*. They didn't feel as if performers should have to compete against each other, especially when they were friends. On July 13th, the CMA people denied their request. On August 20, 1977, the ballots were published, and Waylon was in the lead with five nominations.

Waylon and Willie had been friends for many years and by 1977, they were both at the top of their careers. It was decided that it was time for them to record an album together, an album of duets. That they recorded on two different labels was thought to be a problem. Waylon was on RCA, and Willie was on Columbia. Surprisingly, when Columbia was approached about the project, they agreed almost immediately. The album contains eleven songs by the two artists: three were done individually by each of them as solos, and the remaining five were duets. The album *Waylon and Willie* wasn't released until January of 1978, but the first single was a Waylon solo effort called "The Wurlitzer Prize (I Don't Want to Get Over You)." It was written by the same guys who wrote "Luckenbach, Texas," Moman and Emmons. Now, when I read this title, I didn't remember it. I wasn't that big into country in 1978 (as I explained in the introduction, that didn't come until the Eighties), but the minute I listened to the song, I recognized it. I wonder why they didn't just call it "I Don't Want to Get Over You" as they seem to be the main lyrics in the song. The single was Waylon's sixth number one song, staying at the top two weeks for the weeks November 19th and 26th.

On November 16th, Waylon and Willie got together in the studio and recorded the second single from the album *Waylon and Willie*. "Mamas, Don't Let Your Babies Grow Up to Be Cowboys," was written and recorded by Ed Bruce back in 1975. Bruce reached number fifteen back then, but our two heroes would make it their next number one. It hit the charts on January 28, 1978, got to number one on March 4th, and stayed there for four weeks. It even charted on the pop charts, reaching number 42 on the Billboard Hot 100. The song has really been around. It won a Grammy for Waylon and Willie in 1979 for *Best Country Performance by a Duo or a Group with Vocal.* Willie also used the song as a solo in the movie *Electric Cowboy.* In addition, the *Western Writers of America* named it to their list of the *Top 100 Western Songs of All Time.*

The album *Waylon and Willie* was, of course, another number one album, staying at number one on and off for eleven weeks and staying on the album chart itself for 126 weeks or about 2 ½ years. *Rolling Stone* magazine ranks the album number 30 in its list of the *50 Country Albums Every Rock Fan Should Own.* Not everybody liked *Waylon and Willie* that much. AllMusic said it wasn't great just "good." They said it could have been so much better.

18 - THE END OF THE SEVENTIES

In 1978, Waylon took part in the recording of an interesting album called *White Mansions*. It's really not his album; there were four different performers involved in the recording: Waylon, Jessi Colter, John Dillon, and Steve Cash. Each of them played a different character in the Civil War, and the songs tell their story. It was totally a concept album, and no singles were released from it, but it managed to get to number 38 on the Billboard Country Album charts and just broke through the Billboard Top 200 (which includes all genres) at 181. Waylon says he didn't think most of the people that heard the album understood it, but that he really enjoyed recording it.

He also joined with Johnny Cash to contribute two duets to Cash's album *I Would Like to See You Again*. One of those singles was "There Ain't No Good Chain Gang" which rose to number two on the country charts where it stayed for two weeks. These collaborations with others, like Johnny and Willie Nelson, were a precursor to a super group that would come along in the Eighties. Stay tuned.

By this time, Waylon was tiring of the "Outlaw" image. He and Willie had started it, but now it seemed to have run its course. The next album reflected this change of heart with a single called "Don't You Think This Outlaw Bit's Done Got Out of Hand," which I talked about previously. The single was from the album *I've Always Been Crazy*, released in September 1978. It spent the last eight weeks of the year at the top of the Billboard Country Album charts.

The title song from *I've Always Been Crazy* was Waylon's sixth number one as a solo artist. It stayed at number one for three weeks in September 1978.

One other significant thing about *I've Always Been Crazy* is that Waylon paid tribute to his old friend Buddy Holly. He did a medley of Buddy Holly songs: "Well All Right"/"It's So Easy"/"Maybe Baby"/"Peggy Sue." This medley never made the charts, but it's great to listen to.

In January of 1979, there debuted on television a new show which was called a combination of *Beverly Hillbillies* and *Starsky & Hutch*. The show was *The Dukes of Hazzard* which revolved around two guys who drove a fast car (called the General Lee), a beautiful girl (Catherine Bach) who wore cut-off jeans, and the local sheriff (who was always trying to catch them doing something illegal). Waylon had done a narration job for a movie in 1975 called *Moonrunners*. He still had his radio voice from years before, and CBS was impressed, so they called Waylon and asked him if would do the voice-over for the show. He was the narrator and was eventually called The Balladeer. In Waylon's autobiography, he says he never appeared on camera, but that's not true. In the last season, there was an episode called "Welcome, Waylon" in which he had a cameo. Waylon also wrote the theme song for the show. "Theme from The Dukes of Hazzard (Good Ol' Boys)" hit number one on November 1, 1980 and stayed there for just one week. The version used in the TV show is slightly different from the version recorded for his next album. Waylon was given one of the General Lee cars used in the show as a gift, and he had that car for most of the rest of his life.

In the early hours of May 19, 1979, Waylon and Jessi went to Nashville Baptist Hospital to bring their first and only child into the world. Waylon and Jessi had been trying for years, and time was running short with Jessi being 36 and Waylon, 42. Going into the hospital, they did not know the sex of the baby but, later that day, a baby boy was born. He was healthy with all ten fingers and ten toes. The couple knew a boy from church whose real name was Shooter. When their boy was born, they named him Waylon Albright Jennings (the Albright comes from Richie Albright, Waylon's long-time friend and drummer), but he would always be known as Shooter. Shooter would grow up to be his own man. He followed dad into the business and at last count has about eleven studio albums to his name and several live albums. He hasn't had the success his father had but then who has?

Waylon finished the Seventies with three number one songs in 1979. The first was from his *Greatest Hits* album which was released in April of 1979. The album contained eleven songs, all of which had previously appeared on some album. It has always intrigued me that many times a record company will put new songs on a *Greatest Hits* album. Maybe it's to get the die-hard fans who want everything the performer has ever done and helps sell the *Greatest Hits* album. The one song on this album that was not a "greatest hit" was "Amanda." "Amanda" was written by Bob McDill, but I cannot find if it refers to anyone specific. Don Williams recorded the song in 1973. Waylon recorded it in 1974, and it was included on his *The Ramblin' Man* album. However, it was not released as a single then. Now, in 1979, they took that old recording, added some overdubbing, and came up with a new version of "Amanda" without Waylon having to do a thing. The song was his first number one of 1979 and stayed at the top for three weeks from June 30th until July 14th.

The last album of the decade for Waylon was *What Goes Around Comes Around*. It was his first album since 1975 that did not hit number one, peaking at number two, which is still not bad. It stayed at number two for fourteen weeks, being kept out of the top spot by Kenny Rogers' album *Kenny*. By this time, it was obvious to Waylon, if not to the public, that his time was spent, and that he had peaked. He had two number one singles from the album, however. The first was "Come With Me" which hit the top on November 17th and stayed for two weeks.

The second single from *What Goes Around Comes Around* was "I Ain't Living Long Like This" which was written by Rodney Crowell. The song was covered by several country artists like Gary Stewart and Emmylou Harris, but Waylon's version is the only one that charted, and it went to number one, becoming the eleventh number one single of his career. The song is really a cry for help from Waylon. In 1979, he was at the peak of his cocaine use, and he really wanted to break the habit, but it seemed to have complete control of him.

19 - BROKE

Waylon was in the habit of releasing about one album a year. His album for 1980 was *Music Man,* released on May 20th. It was his fifth number one album in the past six attempts. Unfortunately, it was his last number one album for five years; his next didn't come until 1985.

There were three singles from *Music Man*. The biggest hit was "The Theme from The Dukes of Hazzard (Good Ol' Boys)" which spent a week at number one. Just before that, he released "Clyde" which was written by J.J. Cale. Cale had recorded the song himself, as well as other performers, like Dr Hook. It's a cool song about a man sitting on his porch with his bass guitar and playing the blues. The song peaked at number seven on the country charts.

The third single from *Music Man* was "Storms Never Last" which was written by his wife, Jessi Colter. One day, Jessi came to Waylon and said, "I have a silly song for you." Waylon liked the song but said there wasn't a rhyming line in it. It reached number seventeen on the charts.

AllMusic said this was not a great album, but it was a "good album." Waylon would have difficulty hitting the top spot with an album from then on. In fact, there would only be one more in his career.

On June 9, 1980, something happened which could be called funny or tragic depending on how you look at it. The tragic part is that comedian Richard Pryor got severe burns from freebasing cocaine in Los Angeles. When Waylon was talking to Pryor's wife about the incident, hearing about the burns he received, Waylon offered to donate some of his skin to graft on Pryor. I'm not sure if Pryor's wife laughed or just shook her head but, of course, Pryor is black and Waylon is white. A skin graft from Waylon would be a poor match for a black man.

On October 23, 1980, Waylon had his first network television special. Called "Waylon, Starring Waylon Jennings," guest stars included Jessi Colter and James Garner, the actor.

By 1981, Waylon was on the verge of declaring bankruptcy. Waylon and company were broke. In fact, he was over two and a half million dollars in debt. How could someone who was as successful as Waylon, who had numerous number one records, and who had been on the road playing concerts be broke you ask? The answer could be that he just wasn't paying attention. And the main reason he wasn't passing attention can be summed up in one word: cocaine.

Waylon had dozens of people on his payroll. There were seventeen people working in his Nashville office alone. His road crew was enormous. He had a road manager, a band manager, a publicist, a secretary, a booking agent, a receptionist (not sure what the difference between that and a secretary is, but he had both), people he called "gofers," and several personal assistants. They all had to be paid. By 1981, he was $2 million in debt, and all of his banks (there were sixteen of them) closed his accounts because he was $860,000 overdrawn. Waylon never saw it coming. He said that, on tour, he never left the bus except to go to the hotel and then to the stage. He had no interaction with his staff and relied on others to do all the paperwork. Because of that, a lot of them were robbing him blind. Since Waylon was high, almost all the time, he was oblivious to what was happening all around him until one day his friends Bill Robinson and Richie Albright sat him down and showed him the figures. He said this couldn't go on. Something had to change.

Someone from the IRS told him he could prosecute several of his staff, and they should serve jail time. However, Waylon didn't want to put anyone in jail; he mostly blamed himself and so he just started cleaning house. Most of his staff were fired, and Waylon started all over again. He took two people that he could trust, Marylou and Terry Lawrence (they understood the business), and they moved all of his records to their home and started to work on paying off the debts and making the banks happy again. It took them a year, but Waylon was able to get out from under this burden and did not have to declare bankruptcy. Marylou Lawrence became Waylon's personal assistant.

Waylon lost many friends during this time, the most important being Richie Albright. He didn't really lose him as a friend, they were friends until Waylon's death, but Richie thought it was time to leave the band and so he sort of retired. He had been addicted to cocaine over the past several years like Waylon was, but he knew he needed to get clean and so he left the band so he could concentrate on getting off the drug.

There was only one new album in 1981, maybe because Waylon was busy with his finances. He and Jessi found time to record an album called *Leather and Lace* which was released in February of 1981. The album peaked at number eleven on the country album charts. Most critics say that this album marked the end of the "Outlaw" music that Waylon was known for in the Seventies. Jessi wrote three of the tracks on the album, one being "Storms Never Last" which was also on the *Music Man* album. The only single hit to come from the album was a medley they did of "Wild Side of Life" & "It Wasn't God Who Made Honky Tonk Angels," which was released on May 15, 1981 and reached number ten on the singles charts. "Wild Side of Life" was originally done by Hank Thompson way back in 1952. Later that year, Kitty Wells came out with "It Wasn't God Who Made Honky Tonk Angels" which was an answer song to "Wild Side of Life." Kitty Wells reached number one on the country single charts and, with this song, became the first woman in country music history to have a solo number one hit.

Late in 1981, Waylon reunited with his old producer Chips Moman. They put together his next album, *Black on Black,* which was released on February 9, 1982. The cover of the album shows an all back background with the famous stylised "W" (called the Flying W), standing for Waylon. Moman now had his own studios in Nashville, and that's where this album was recorded. *Black on Black* was panned by some critics, but the public loved it enough to get it to number three on the album charts. Some say that Waylon was trying too hard to get away from the "Outlaw" image, that these songs just didn't have any substance. The album produced three hit singles, the first being "Shine" which was written by Waylon and peaked at number five. The song was used in the closing credits of the movie *The Pursuit of D.B.Cooper*.

The second single from *Black on Black* was "Just to Satisfy You" which Waylon had recorded back in 1963. While it was a local Phoenix hit, it never hit the national charts. This time, he got together with his friend Willie Nelson, and they recorded the song as a duet. It was released in February of 1982 and swiftly rose to number one on the singles chart on May 22nd, where it stayed for two weeks.

The third single from *Black on Black* was "Women Do Know How to Carry On." There's not much to say about this song. It was written by Waylon and Bobby Emmons, who co-wrote "Luckenbach, Texas." It was released June 26, 1982, and it peaked at number four on the singles charts.

1982 ended with the release of the album *WW II* on September 30th. I'm assuming the WW stands for Waylon and Willie, not World War. The album peaked at number three on the album chart, and there was only one single from the album, "Sittin' On the Dock of the Bay" which, as you probably already know, was a cover of the 1968 Otis Redding song. The song was written by Redding and a fellow named Steve Cropper. It was recorded just six days before Redding was killed in a plane crash. The song was released posthumously and was the biggest hit of Otis Redding's career. It was also the first hit on the pop charts to hit number one after the death of the performer.

The album *WW II* did not live up to the popularity of its predecessor, *Waylon and Willie.*

On January 17, 1983, Waylon recorded the first of two singles which would come from his next album. That album was *It's Only Rock & Roll,* and the single was "Lucille (You Won't Do Your Daddy's Will)". "Lucille" was, of course, the classic rock-and-roll song from Little Richard which peaked at number 21 on the pop charts back in 1957. Waylon did much better than that, taking the song to number one on the country charts. I have to admit, I was taken back a little when I heard Waylon's version of this song. Somehow, I expected him to scream out the lyrics like Little Richard did, but his version is mellow and almost a ballad. I still like it, however. Waylon had only two more number ones coming in his career.

The other single from *It's Only Rock & Roll* was called "Breakin' Down" which was written by Joe Rainey and just made the Top 10 by peaking at number ten.

It's Only Rock & Roll was released on May 31, 1983 and peaked at number ten on the album charts. It was Waylon's worst showing since 1975 when *Honky Tonk Heroes* only got to number fourteen.

In April of 1983, Waylon got together with Willie Nelson for a third time. This was a duet album called *Take It to the Limit,* even though a lot of the songs were done by either Waylon or Willie. One exception to this was "Take It to the Limit," the title song. The title on the record actually says "Willie Nelson with Waylon Jennings," so it relegates Waylon to second place in the collaboration. The album peaked at number three on the album chart, and the single went to number eight. The single is, of course, a remake of the Eagles song which was a number four song on the pop chart in 1975.

The rest of 1983 was business as usual. Waylon was so deep into cocaine that he sometimes didn't know where he was or what he should be doing. In September, he released his second album that year called *Waylon and Company*. This was another album of duets like he had done before, but this time the duets were all with different people. The album itself did just a little worse than *It's Only Rock & Roll*, peaking at number twelve. Waylon was starting to lose momentum, and he knew it. *Waylon and Company* did produce four Top 20 singles but in the past, those would have all been Top 10 singles.

The first of those three singles was "Hold On, I'm Comin'," which was a duet with Jerry Reed. This is another cover of a song from the pop or soul charts. It was originally done by Sam and Dave back in 1967. The original peaked at number one on the R&B charts and at number 21 on the pop charts. Waylon and Jerry Reed's version went to number twenty in 1983.

The second song from *Waylon and Company* was a single that was recorded on August 5, 1982 by Hank Williams Jr. and Waylon Jennings with an assist from Ernest Tubb. The song was called "Leave Them Boys Alone," and it wasn't released until May of 1983. It reached number six on the country charts and is usually listed under Hank Williams Jr. The reason I mention it here is that Waylon took part in the record and, more importantly, this was the last time Ernest Tubb ever recorded a song. Ernest Tubb was 68 years old when he recorded the song and died just two years later, in 1984.

The third song from *Waylon and Company* was "The Conversation," which was a duet between Waylon and Hank Williams Jr. The song was originally released on Williams' 1979 album *Whiskey Bent and Hell Bound*. The song was re-released for Waylon's album, and he got a number fifteen hit from it. When Hank Williams Jr.'s album was released in 1979, one reviewer thought the song was OK. The best he could say about it was that, "It didn't make you gag." Faint praise, indeed.

The fourth and final song from *Waylon and Company* was "I May Be Used (But Baby I Ain't Used Up)," a song that wasn't released until

March 3, 1984, even though it had been recorded almost a year earlier on July 18, 1983. Of all the hits coming from *Waylon and Company,* this one did the best, peaking at number four.

20 - GETTING RID OF THE DEMONS

In February of 1984, Waylon performed a two-night stand with Gary Morris at the Los Angeles Universal Amphitheater. At some point during that two-day period, Johnny Cash came and visited with him. Johnny had just finished a stay at the Betty Ford Clinic, and he encouraged Waylon to get off of cocaine.

It took another month before Waylon took that seriously and took steps to quit the drug. He had the money to go into a program or join a rehab center for help in kicking the addiction but instead he decided to do it alone. Not many people can do that and be successful, but Waylon was.

Before that, however, he recorded another album called *Never Could Toe the Mark*. This was one of the last albums he recorded for RCA as his album (and singles) were not selling as well as they had. *Never Could Toe the Mark* peaked at number twenty on the album charts, and the title song, "Never Could Toe the Mark," got to number six on the singles charts. The single wasn't released until June 16th, which was just about the time the album was released.

Waylon knew it was time to quit, but he wouldn't say the words out loud. He told Jessi that he was going to "stop" and that, maybe at some future time, he might take up the habit again. He took the month of April of 1984 off from recording and touring and rented a house in the middle of nowhere in the desert of Arizona, somewhere near Phoenix. He and Jessi moved into the rented house and there they stayed for the month of April.

Waylon doesn't talk much about why he felt now was the time to get cleaned up. He does leave one clue, however, which I am inclined to believe might have been the turning point. Waylon never did drugs in front of his son, Shooter. Shooter was about five when Waylon started his rehab. Sometime in the year before that, Waylon walked into a room where Shooter was, and the boy had picked up a straw and was putting it to his nose and sniffing it. This is exactly how cocaine users ingest the drug. Of course, Shooter didn't get any drugs, it was just an empty straw, but this affected Waylon as he didn't think Shooter knew anything about his habit. I have no proof of this, but I believe that was the turning point for Waylon.

Waylon drove his bus up into the driveway of the rented house and parked it. On the night of March 31, 1984, he stayed on the bus and, literally, took in as much cocaine as he could tolerate. He then left the remains (about $20,000 worth) on the bus and went into the house. His intention was that the drug was there, just waiting outside. If he needed it, he could get it. However, he knew he could get through this on his own. He went "cold turkey."

I remember a time when I was younger and was very overweight. I had joined Weight Watchers and was headed for my first meeting. I stopped at a restaurant before I went to the meeting and ordered enough food for two meals. I knew that after I left the WW meeting, I would be restricted on what I could eat, and I wanted to fill up on food that I might not eat for a while. That is almost exactly what Waylon did. One last high before he goes into self-imposed rehab. Unlike Waylon, who was successful, I stayed on Weight Watchers for a month or so and then just went back to my old habits. Waylon, on the other hand, never went out to that bus and never touched that cocaine.

It was a tough month for him. A doctor came and gave him vitamin shots but otherwise he was on his own. He said he felt like somebody had pulled the plug. He had convulsions, and he says he was constantly filled with anticipation. His bones hurt; his whole body was a mass of pain. He couldn't sleep. If it hadn't been for Jessi, he might not have made it. She was there every second of the time. She never left his side. He says he had to learn how to feel all over again. The drug had stripped away all of his emotions. He ended up eating a lot and gained about 25 pounds during that month. In the end, he made it.

At the end of the month, Waylon walked out of that house a new man. He felt strong and drug free. Then, he thought of the $20,000 worth of cocaine in the bus, and he and Jessi drove out in the desert and flushed it down the bus toilet. They had never been happier.

It wasn't easy getting off drugs. They haunted him for as long as he lived, but I don't think he ever relapsed. He says that now and then, he found a stash in his home or in his bus. A small package that had been overlooked. He says the temptation was always there. It was just about this time that crack was becoming popular. Crack cocaine is in a solid form rather than a powder. It is smoked, usually, and the high comes much faster than with cocaine. It is also much cheaper. It was just a couple weeks after Waylon got clean that someone offered him crack for the first time. He had the strength to turn him down, and he was so glad to be free of the drug, he says he's not sure what would have happened to him if he had taken up crack. But, like I said, it was not easy. It took him eight years before he felt like a normal person again, felt like he could write a song and perform without being high. The after effects went on and on.

On August 1, 1984, Waylon played one of the friends in the video shoot for Hank Williams Jr's song "All My Rowdy Friends Are Coming Over Tonight." It is a great video which you should look up if you haven't seen it.

In October of 1984, RCA released Waylon's second Greatest Hits album called *Waylon's Greatest Hits II*. It was composed of mostly songs that had been popular since they released the first Greatest Hits album. The album stalled at number 27 on the album charts, not even coming close to its predecessor which had hit number one. There were three songs that were new, however. "Looking for Suzanne,"

"America," and "Waltz Me to Heaven." They released the latter two as singles, "America" on September 20th and "Waltz Me to Heaven" on January 19, 1985. Sammy Johns, who was a country music songwriter, wrote "America." There was a video filmed of the song which I remember seeing in the mid-Eighties. The song reached number six on the singles chart. Waylon says "America" was his "farewell anthem for RCA." He was ready to leave and when his contract came up in 1985, he didn't sign it and went with MCA instead.

The second song from the *Greatest Hits II* album was "Waltz Me to Heaven" which was written by Dolly Parton. While Waylon recorded the song as a single, which reached number ten on the charts, the song was also featured in the movie *Rhinestone* which starred Dolly Parton and Sylvester Stallone. In the movie, Floyd Parton, who was Dolly's younger brother, sang the song.

21 - THE HIGHWAYMEN

On November 12, 1984, Waylon joined with a few of his friends in Montreux, Switzerland to tape a Christmas special due to air in December. Johnny Cash was the headliner, and the show was called *Johnny Cash: Christmas on the Road.* Also starring in the special were Waylon, Willie, and Kris Kristofferson, along with two of their wives: June Carter Cash and Jessi Colter. Now, Johnny Cash did a Christmas special almost every year in the Seventies and Eighties. Several of them can be found on YouTube in their entirety. In 1984, he asked his three friends to join him on the show. This was significant because they were just about the last of the singers that were known for being a part of the Outlaw movement.

During the taping of this show, the four guys decided that they enjoyed singing together. This was fun. They did the show and then went home to Nashville, got together, and started recording an album. Today, we call them a super group. This was the start of The Highwaymen, but to them they were just four friends getting together doing what they loved. At first, they did not even have a name. Marty Stuart, who later became a headlining act himself, played guitar on the album. Stuart hit the Top 40 in 1985 but didn't become a real star until the Nineties.

They later called themselves The Highwaymen, after a song written by Jimmy Webb in 1977 for his album *El Mirage.* The song was not a hit for Jimmy Webb, but the four guys knew of it and thought it perfect for them. The song is based on the life of Jonathan Wild, a London criminal who worked both sides of the law, claiming to be a crime-fighter while stealing whatever he could. He was eventually hanged. They changed the name slightly, and "Highwayman" was their first single from the album of the same name.

The song describes four different people: first was the highwayman who robbed stagecoaches, sung by Willie. Next came a sailor who risks his life on the open sea and falls in and drowns, sung by Kris Kristofferson. The third is a construction worker working on building the Hoover Dam who falls to his death, sung by Waylon. Lastly, there is the captain of the starship who goes off into space and never comes back, sung by Johnny Cash. The most moving part of the song is that they are all gone, but they still remain, and they will come back again (and again and again....). That gives me chills every time I hear it. The single was number one on the country charts for one week during the week of August 17th. An interesting side note is that there are 52 weeks in a year. During 1985, 51 different songs hit number one. No one stayed there more than a week except Ronnie Milsap who stayed at number one for two weeks with his hit "Lost in the Fifties."

In January of 1985, Waylon was asked to be a part of the celebrity group *USA for Africa*. There were originally 44 artists asked to record a song that was a relief effort for the famine that was running rampant in Africa. The idea came from the English group Band Aid who had recorded "Do They Know It's Christmas" the previous December. The song "We Are the World" was a great and moving song and featured almost every big name that was recording in 1985. Waylon was there in the beginning, but somewhere along the way, he got fed up with it and left the recording. His voice is still heard on the record, however. Today, as I study the video of "We Are the World," I cannot find Waylon in the group, so I have to assume he wasn't included in the filming. Remember, this was just a couple months before he started his self-imposed rehab in Arizona.

The Highwaymen recorded three albums together. The first was just called *Highwayman* and was released in May of 1985. It was credited to Nelson/Jennings/Cash/Kristofferson. The name "The Highwaymen" did not come along until later. The album spent one week at number one the week of September 28, 1985. They released a second single from that first album called "Desperados Waiting for a Train," written by Guy Clark. It peaked at number fifteen on the charts. It had been recorded by many country artists before our four heroes did it, and it was recorded afterwards as well.

The second album was called *Highwayman 2*. Released February 9, 1990, it reached number four on the album chart. Three singles were released from that album, but none of them reached the Top 20. "Silver Stallion" reached number 25, but the other two, "Born and Raised in Black and White" and "American Remains," did not chart at all.

Their third album was called *The Road Goes on Forever* and was the first time The Highwaymen was used as the name of their group. It was released on April 4, 1995 and peaked at number 42. It looked like the Highwaymen were done.

As soon as they took on the name of The Highwaymen, they got sued by another group called The Highwaymen. The older group were a folk quartet who had had a number one song on the pop charts in 1961 called "Michael" as in "Michael Row the Boat Ashore." They didn't like it that our country friends were using their name. Waylon says the four of them were performing in a television special as the newly named The Highwaymen, so they invited the original group to be on the show, and that mended everything. The lawsuit was dropped, and everyone went their way.

There was just one single from *The Road Goes on Forever*. It was called "It Is What It Is," but it did not chart. By 1985, things were beginning to slow down for Waylon. He was just as busy, he still recorded, and he still toured, but he wasn't being played on the radio like he had before. He had three Top 10 records: "Waltz Me to Heaven," "Highwayman," and "Drinkin' and Dreamin'."

"Drinkin' and Dreamin'," written by Troy Seals and Max D. Barnes, was a single from the album *Turn the Page*. *Turn the Page* was the first album in twenty years that Waylon recorded totally drug free. One critic said that it seemed like Waylon was celebrating his sobriety. The album only made it to 23 on the album chart, but Waylon was happy with it. As usual, he covered some hits by other performers, like the title song "Turn the Page" by Bob Seger and "Rhiannon" from Stevie Nicks. The single "Drinkin' and Dreamin'" reached number two on the singles chart.

On August 16, 1985, the very last episode of "Dukes of Hazzard" aired on CBS Television. Waylon sang the theme song for the very last time.

Waylon's next album was *Sweet Mother Texas*, released in February of 1986. It was his last album for RCA before moving to MCA. It only had eight songs on it, and the version on YouTube shows that the album timed out at about 28 minutes. That's a very short album and, since there was not much new on the album, it failed to chart at all. It was a sad ending to Waylon's career with RCA.

22 - CHANGING LABELS

Sometimes changing labels can be the spark an artist needs to get back on top. He was with new people and got renewed motivation. His first album with MCA was *Will the Wolf Survive,* released March 10, 1986. It reached number one on the album chart. It was his first number one solo album since *Music Man* in 1980.

Will the Wolf Survive was a short come back for Waylon. Not only did the album hit number one, but three singles from the album all hit the Top 10. The first of those was "Working Without a Net." Released on February 15, 1986, it reached number seven on the country chart. Second was the title song "Will the Wolf Survive," which was a cover of the song recorded by the Chicano Rock group Los Lobos. They hit number 26 on the Billboard Hot Rock Tracks chart in 1984. Waylon made it to number five on the country chart. The third single was "What You'll Do When I'm Gone," written by Larry Butler, and was released on September 20, 1986. It peaked at number eight.

On May 18, 1986, CBS Television broadcast a remake of the classic movie *Stagecoach*. The popularity of The Highwaymen influenced them to cast Waylon, Willie, Johnny, and Kris in the film. Also in the movie were John Schneider from "The Dukes of Hazzard" and the two wives: Jessi Colter and June Carter Cash. Kris Kristofferson played the Ringo Kid, the part played by John Wayne in the 1939 original. Willie played Doc Holliday, and Waylon played a gambler named Hatfield. Johnny Cash was Marshall Curly Wilcox.

On September 10, 1986, Waylon recorded "Rose in Paradise" which was released on January 12, 1987. It was included on his next album for MCA called *Hangin' Tough* (not to be confused with an album by the same name from Backstreet Boys). *Hangin' Tough*, released in January of 1987, only went to number nineteen, but the first single,

"Rose in Paradise," was a number one single, hitting the top the week of April 25th. Alas, "Rose in Paradise" was the last number one Waylon ever had. "Rose" is a woman who marries a banker who was humble and caring before they married but who turns into a control freak afterwards. The banker hires a gardener to watch Rose and one day she disappears. Was she killed or did she run away with the gardener? We will never know. The song stayed on the charts for nineteen weeks.

The second single from *Hangin' Tough* was "Fallin' Out," another song about a troubled marriage which was released on May 16, 1987. It reached number eight on the singles chart.

Waylon knew that his star was beginning to dim. His career had peaked, and he could sort of look forward to retirement. Of course, performers never really retire; they just stop hitting the charts. After *Hangin' Tough*, he recorded an album called *A Man Called Hoss*. Every song on this album was written by Waylon and his friend Roger Murrah. This album is billed as an "audio-biography." It starts with a Prologue in which Waylon explains the concept of the album. Each "chapter" or cut on the album represents a part of his life. Chapter 1 is about his birth and bringing up in Littlefield, Texas. Chapter 2 is about being a Texan: "You'll Never Take the Texas Out of Me." And so forth. He has a chapter on drugs and a couple on his loves, both lost and found. The album was released October 19, 1987 and reached number 22 on the album chart. Not spectacular, but I did say his star was dimming.

Here might be a good spot to talk about Waylon's nicknames. The first mention I can find of Waylon being called "Hoss" was when Richie Albright was trying to switch Waylon from the pills Waylon was taking to cocaine. Richie said, "Look, Hoss, try this." Waylon did, and the rest is drug history. Richie calling him Hoss kind of stuck. When he was a little kid, his father used to call him "towhead" because back then his hair was a lighter color. When the band was young, the band members used to call him Waymore, after Waymore Svenson, a Swiss yodeler. Sometimes, just for fun, they called him Penrod Jenkins, and nobody really knows why. Waylon liked to call Hank Williams Jr. "Bocephus" which was a nickname Hank's father had given him and became well-known in the country music world. In return, Hank called Waylon "Watashi," Japanese for "old number one."

There were two singles released from *A Man Called Hoss*. The first was "My Rough and Rowdy Days," which was chapter six on the album. The song was released on August 24, 1987 and peaked at number six on the chart.

The second single from *A Man Called Hoss* was "If Ole Hank Could Only See Us Now," a fun song about how things have changed since Hank Williams was recording. Waylon talks about all the technology that has occurred since the time Hank was active. The song was chapter five on the album, released on January 3, 1988, and peaked at number sixteen.

23 - HEART SURGERY

Waylon never took care of himself. By 1988, he was off drugs, and he had quit smoking (six packs a day), but the years he had taken drugs were taking a toll on his body. He was a heavy smoker for much of his life. Therefore, it shouldn't have surprised him when in October of 1988, while he was playing at the *Crazy Horse Steak House* in Santa Ana, California, he suddenly started getting pains in his arms. Jessi massaged them, and the pain went away temporarily, but the next day the pain had moved to his lungs. He says that it felt like his lungs were full of water.

They took him to the hospital, and the doctors decided he needed an angioplasty, a procedure where they insert a small balloon into your arteries, inflate it, and break away any blood clots. Unfortunately, for some reason, it didn't work on Waylon. They gave him an $8000 pill and sent him back to the hotel. After this, Waylon felt fine, so they finished their commitments and returned to Nashville.

A few weeks later, in December, they were leaving Nashville to go to another concert in Bristol, Tennessee, when about twenty miles out of town, Waylon started getting bad chest pains. They turned around, went back to Nashville, and checked into a hospital. Turns out he had not had a heart attack; at least, not yet. The doctors told him he needed a heart bypass, and not just one, but four. Waylon considered his options, including how it would take him off the road for a time, and decided to go ahead and do the surgery. The newspapers say he had a triple bypass, but in his autobiography, he says it was all four.

There's a story that Waylon tells in his autobiography which I like and want to share with you, the reader. I will paraphrase the story. The night he was to undergo surgery, the Dallas Cowboys were playing the San Francisco 49ers. Waylon had bet his friend, Bill Robertson,

$20 that Dallas would win. Just before they rolled Waylon into surgery, Robertson came up to him (he's lying on the gurney) and says something to the effect that San Francisco was ahead and probably would win the game. He thought maybe Waylon should give the $20 to a neutral person to hold in case something bad happened during the surgery. Waylon says he laughed loud and long.

Needless to say, Waylon survived and lived another thirteen years or so. An amazing coincidence is that Johnny Cash had the exact same problem at the same time and, for a short time, was in a bed right next to Waylon. He also had to get a bypass and, of course, he also lived through it with no lasting effects.

By 1989, Shooter was ten years old and beginning to ask questions and looking for help with his schoolwork. Waylon couldn't answer all of them, but it gave him the motivation to set an example for all of his kids, not just Shooter. He was 54 years old and had never graduated from high school. He didn't want any of his kids to make that mistake, so he studied and took the GED test, passing it. He received his certificate on January 29, 1990 at the state capitol of Kentucky, Frankfort.

The rest of the Eighties were rather uneventful for Waylon. He kept doing what he had always been doing. He hosted the television show *Hee Haw* a couple times and still toured when he could. The charts would remain elusive to him until 1990.

In 1990, Waylon was welcomed into the cornfield on the television show *Hee Haw*. That was a distinct honor. Those of you who have seen the show know the camera opens on a cornfield, then someone pops up (like whack-a-mole) and tells a joke or a one-liner. Waylon got to do that as a guest on the show. The entire cornfield set was based on the "Joke Wall" on the *Rowan & Martin's Laugh In* show.

The decade of the Nineties can be summed up in one word: "Wrong." This single was the last that Waylon would record that made it to the

Top 10. "Wrong" comes from an album called *The Eagle. The Eagle* was released on June 29, 1990 and was also his last album to make the Top 10, peaking at number nine. Although "Wrong" was written by Steve Seskin and Andre Pessis, the title of the song goes back almost to the beginning of Waylon's career.

Jerry Groop was one of the original Waylors, back in the Sixties when Waylon was trying to get a break. He was a left-handed guitar player, and he always stood to the left of Waylon so that his guitar was pointed right at him. Waylon says that every time he (Waylon) made a mistake, hit a wrong note or said a lyric that was incorrect, Groop would mutter, "Wrong" to Waylon. It was only loud enough for Waylon to hear it, but he heard it many times in the early days. That was the genesis of his last Top 10 single. "Wrong" hit the charts on June 26, 1990 and peaked at number five.

The Highwaymen were active through much of the Nineties. If it hadn't been for that group, Waylon probably would have faded from sight much earlier than he did. On October 10, 1990, the Discovery Space Shuttle returned to earth, and the crew's wake-up call that morning was the guys' recording of "The Highwayman," especially the part, "I fly a starship."

In 1992, *Country American* magazine listed its *Top 100 Country Songs of All-Time.* Waylon has two on the list: "Amanda" at number 68 and "Theme From Dukes of Hazard (Good Ol' Boys)," at number 96.

In 1993, we went to space again, and "Mammas Don't Let Your Babies Grow Up To Be Cowboys" woke up the crew of the Endeavor Space Shuttle.

In 1994, Waylon did a cameo on the television show *Married...With Children*, playing a character named Ironhead Haynes. He was also in the movie *Maverick* starring Mel Gibson, James Garner, and Jodie Foster that year, playing "man with concealed guns."

James Hoag

Littlefield, Texas, where Waylon was born, named September 3, 1995 "Waylon Jennings Day." Johnny Cash was there, and the two celebrated the day.

As we get closer to 2002, there is less and less to tell about Waylon. He tried to keep going, performing when he could. But, in 1995, he cancelled eleven shows after seeing the doctor and being told he had a "variety of ailments." Late in 1995, he and others were inducted into the Nashville *Songwriters Hall of Fame* and on October 6, he played at The Surf Ballroom in Clear Lake, Iowa, the place where he had played bass for Buddy Holly all those years before. This was the first time he had been back since that fateful night in 1959. His life had officially come full circle. In 1997, Waylon continued to cancel shows, following doctor's orders.

In January of 1999, he found the strength to get together with Willie Nelson, Kris Kristofferson, and Travis Tritt to star in a CBS television movie called *Outlaw Justice*. They changed the official name of the movie to *The Long Kill* and site IMDB describes the movie this way: "Two aging gunfighters (Nelson, Kristofferson) re-form their old gang to avenge the murder of one of the former members."

Late in 1999, Waylon visited the home of Robbie Turner, a steel guitarist who had been with Waylon in the early days, and they recorded the tracks for the last album Waylon ever made. The album was called *Goin' Down Rockin': The Last Recordings*, and it wasn't released until September of 2012. The album wasn't completed when Waylon died, and the family didn't want to release any posthumous recordings, feeling like the record company was just taking advantage of his name. Robby Turner owned rights to the recordings, since he had played on them. Overruling the family, he released the album in 2012. It peaked at number fourteen on the country album charts.

On January 5, 2000, Waylon played the Ryman Auditorium in Nashville for the last time. He sang a duet with Travis Tritt called

"I've Always Been Crazy." Montgomery Gentry joined him on "I'm a Ramblin' Man."

After years of drugs and smoking, even though he had quit both, his body was beginning to fail him. He had acquired diabetes and in April of 2000, he had surgery in Phoenix to reduce arterial blockage in his legs. Waylon decided to move back to Arizona, where he still owned a home. In late 2000, he started selling off everything he owned in Nashville that wouldn't make any sense to take to Arizona. One thing he sold was the General Lee, the Dodge Charger they had given him for his work on *The Dukes of Hazzard*. The car sold for $45,000.

On October 4, 2001, they inducted Waylon into the *Country Music Hall of Fame*. At the time, Waylon said he didn't care about the award. He didn't even go to the ceremony. Instead, he sent one of his kids to accept the award.

Time was running out for Waylon. On November 13, 2001, he went again to a hospital in Phoenix for surgery for vascular disease. Several shows were cancelled because of that. On December 19, 2001, they amputated his left foot as the diabetes was getting worse and worse.

He left the hospital on January 7, 2002 and just one month and five days later, on February 12, 2002, Waylon Jennings passed away quietly in his sleep at his home in Chandler, Arizona. The official cause of death was diabetes. He was 64 years old.

There was a memorial service just three days later for Waylon on February 15th, and Jessi Colter, his wife of over 32 years, sang the song she had written all those years ago, "Storms Never Last." He was buried in *The City of Mesa Cemetery* in Mesa, Arizona. The grave is well-marked and if you are in the area, I would assume you could visit the grave. It is a private cemetery, but it seems to be open to the public.

24 - THE LEGACY OF WAYLON JENNINGS

Three days after his death, a group of his friends got together at the Ryman Auditorium for the Grand Ole Opry and performed a show they called "This One's For Waylon." Hank Williams Jr. performed at the Opry for the first time in 20 years. Travis Tritt and Marty Stuart also performed, and Master of Ceremonies Porter Wagoner used the entire broadcast to honor the songs of Waylon Jennings. That show is available on YouTube. There are seven parts to the show, and it will take you about an hour to watch them all.

Just a month after that first show at the Ryman, on March 23rd, they did it again with another tribute to Waylon. Taking part were Hank Williams Jr., Kris Kristofferson, David Lee Murphy, Billy Ray Cyrus, Travis Tritt, and Charley Pride.

It took them one year to get the marker made for his burial plot. They installed it on March 15, 2003. It's a flat marble block that lies even with the ground, not a standing gravestone. It says, "Waylon Jennings, June 15, 1937 - Feb 13, 2002, I am my beloved, My beloved is mine, A loving Son, Husband, Father, and Grandfather." It also says he was a "vagabond dreamer" and a "revolutionary in country music."

Also, in March, the *Country Music Foundation* published a book called *Heartaches By The Number*, which includes the 500 Greatest Singles in country music. The book is available on Amazon. Waylon has five entries in the book, three of which are "Amanda," "Only Daddy That'll Walk the Line," and "Good Hearted Woman." Then, also in March, the CMA lists the *40 Greatest Men of Country Music*, with Waylon coming in at number 5.

If you like lists, then here is another one. In June of 2003, CMT published its *100 Greatest Songs of Country Music*. Waylon and Willie were on the list twice with "Mammas Don't Let Your Babies Grow Up to Be Cowboys" at number 10 and "Good Hearted Woman" at number 76. It surprised me that none of Waylon's solo efforts made the list. Next year, in 2004, another CMT list called the *100 Greatest Love Songs* premiered on June 13th, and Waylon was number 92 with "Amanda." Again, he hit with Willie and "Good Hearted Woman" at number 68.

Following in his father's footsteps, Shooter Jennings released his first album called *Put the O Back in Country* on March 1, 2005. It reached number 22 on the country album charts. It took Jessi three years to brave the public again. In October 2005, she joined with the Waylors Band for a concert in Franklin, Tennessee. It was the first time they had played together since Waylon's death. Richie Albright was back along with Robby Turner and Barny and Carter Roberson.

In November, they released the movie *Walk the Line*, a biopic of Johnny Cash's life. Johnny had died in 2003. In a brilliant feat of casting, Shooter played the part of his father, Waylon, in the movie.

In 2007, the *Grammy Hall of Fame* inducted the album *Wanted! The Outlaws*. Then the *Academy of Country Music* (ACM) presented the *Cliffie Stone Pioneer Award* to Waylon, along with Dolly Parton and Don Williams. Cliffie Stone was a singer, producer, and musical publisher in the early days of country music. He was active mainly in the Forties and Fifties and is recognized as the person who introduced country music to California.

A year later, in 2008, Waymore's Outlaws were introduced to the world. They were a Waylon Jennings tribute band and right there on drums was our old friend Richie Albright.

In 2016, PBS showed a new documentary which I had the good fortune to see when it was first broadcast. *"American Masters -- The*

Highwaymen: Friends Till the End" debuted on May 27th and contained footage of the four guys, both together as The Highwaymen and apart as solo artists. Most of it is from a concert in 1990 on Long Island, New York. On May 25, 2018, "Outlaws & Armadillos: Country's Roaring '70s" opened at the *Country Music Hall of Fame* in Nashville. It is an exhibit which celebrated the bond between Nashville and Austin, Texas with artifacts which represent Waylon Jennings, Willie Nelson, David Allen Coe, Bobby Bare, and many others. The exhibit is scheduled to be at the Hall of Fame through February 21, 2021 so, depending on when you are reading this, it may still be available to visit.

Waylon recorded sixty albums during his career and had sixteen songs hit the top of the country charts. Few can say that. For someone who started out and stayed a rebel most of his life, he did pretty well for himself. He always did things his own way and, because of his success, he got his way in almost everything he did. This is a tribute to one of the Legends of Country Music - Waylon Jennings.

AFTERWORD

I have had so much fun writing about Waylon Jennings. Anyone who reads my stuff knows that I am not an expert on these people, just a fan (fanatic) who loves music and enjoys telling other people about these artists. As I mentioned before, I did not become acquainted with country music until the early Eighties, and I had to spend some time catching up. Waylon had peaked by that time, and they were playing his music as oldies. I worked for a couple years at a local country radio station and while they played mostly the current stuff, I got a chance to play Waylon once in a while. I recognized right away what a talent he was, and I fell in love with his songs and, especially, his attitude about life, love, and country music.

If he had lived, Waylon Jennings would be 82 this year (2019). Willie Nelson is four years older than Waylon, and he is still performing and appearing in movies so if Waylon could have remained healthy, there's no reason he couldn't still be performing today. Alas, that didn't happen, and we have lost a great performer and a great person. I hope you have enjoyed reading about Waylon Jennings, and I hope you took advantage to listen to some of his music as you made this journey.

ABOUT THE AUTHOR

James Hoag has always been a big fan of Rock & Roll. Most people graduate from high school and then proceed to "grow up" and go on to more adult types of music. James got stuck at about age 18 and has been an avid fan of popular music ever since. His favorite music is from the Fifties, the origin of Rock & Roll and which was the era in which James grew up. But he likes almost all types of popular music including country music.

In 1980, he became friends with a man who introduced him to Country Music and he has been a strong fan of that genre of music ever since.

After working his entire life as a computer programmer, he is now retired, and he decided to share his love of the music and of the performers by writing books that discuss the life and music of the various people who have meant so much to him over the years.

He calls each book a "love letter" to the stars that have enriched our lives so much. These people are truly Legends.

SELECTED DISCOGRAPHY

STUDIO ALBUMS

1964 - Waylon at JD's

1966 - Folk-Country

1966 - Leavin' Town

1966 - Nashville Rebel (soundtrack)

1967 - Waylon Sings Ol' Harlan

1967 - Love of the Common People

1967 - The One and Only

1968 - Hangin' On

1968 - Only the Greatest

1968 - Jewels

1969 - Just to Satisfy You

1970 - Waylon

1970 - Singer of Sad Songs

1971 - The Taker/Tulsa

1971 - Cedartown, Georgia

1972 - Good Hearted Woman

1972 - Ladies Love Outlaws

1973 - Lonesome, On'ry and Mean

1973 - Honky Tonk Heroes

1974 - This Time

1974 - The Ramblin' Man

1975 - Dreaming My Dreams

1976 - Are You Ready for the Country

1977 - Ol' Waylon

1978 - I've Always Been Crazy

1979 - What Goes Around Comes Around

1980 - Music Man

1982 - Black on Black

1983 - It's Only Rock + Roll

1983 - Waylon and Company

1984 - Never Could Toe the Mark

1985 - Turn the Page

1986 - Sweet Mother Texas

1986 - Will the Wolf Survive

1987 - Hangin' Tough

1987 - A Man Called Hoss

1988 - Full Circle

1990 - The Eagle

1992 - Too Dumb for New York City, Too Ugly for L.A.

1992 - Ol' Waylon Sings Ol' Hank

1993 - Cowboys, Sisters, Rascals & Dirt

1994 - Waymore's Blues (Part II)

1996 - Right for the Time

1998 - Closing In on the Fire

2012 - Goin' Down Rockin': The Last Recordings

Collaborations - With Willie Nelson

1978 - Waylon & Willie

1982 - WWII

1983 - Take It to the Limit

1991 - Clean Shirt

1999 - Waylon and Willie Super Hits

Other collaborations

1969 - Country-Folk (with The Kimberlys)

1970 - Ned Kelly (soundtrack)

1976 - Mackintosh & T.J. (soundtrack)

1976 - Wanted! The Outlaws (with Willie Nelson, Jessi Colter and Tompall Glaser)

1978 - White Mansions (with Jessi Colter, John Dillon and Steve Cash)

1982 - Leather and Lace (with Jessi Colter)

1986 - Heroes (with Johnny Cash)

1998 - Old Dogs (with Bobby Bare, Jerry Reed, Mel Tillis)

2004 - The Crickets and Their Buddies (with The Crickets and various artists)

2008 - Waylon Forever (with Shooter Jennings and The .357's)

2013 - Old 97's & Waylon Jennings (with Old 97's)

SINGLES

1959 - "Jole Blon"

1961 - "Another Blue Day"

1962 - "Crying"

1963 - "My Baby Walks All Over Me"

1964 - "Love Denied"

1964 - "Four Strong Winds"

1964 - "Sing the Girls a Song Bill"

1965 - "I Don't Believe You"

1965 - "That's the Chance I'll Have to Take"

1965 - "Stop the World (And Let Me Off)"

1965 - "Anita, You're Dreaming"

1966 - "Time to Bum Again"

1966 - "(That's What You Get) For Lovin' Me"

1966 - "Green River"

1967 - "Mental Revenge"

1967 - "The Chokin' Kind"

1967 - "Walk On Out of My Mind"

1968 - "I Got You" (with Anita Carter)

1968 - "Only Daddy That'll Walk the Line"

1968 - "Yours Love"

1968 - "My World"

1968 - "Another Blue Day"

1969 - "Something's Wrong in California"

1969 - "The Days of Sand and Shovels"

1969 - "Brown Eyed Handsome Man"

1970 - "Singer of Sad Songs"

1970 - "The Taker"

1970 - "(Don't Let the Sun Set on You) Tulsa"

1971 - "Mississippi Woman"

1971 - "Cedartown, Georgia"

1971 - "Good Hearted Woman"

1972 - "Sweet Dream Woman"

1972 - "Pretend I Never Happened"

1973 - "You Can Have Her"

1973 - "We Had It All"

1973 - "You Ask Me To"

1974 - "This Time"

1974 - "I'm a Ramblin' Man"

1975 - "Rainy Day Woman"

1975 - "Dreaming My Dreams with You"

1975 - "Are You Sure Hank Done It This Way"

1976 - "Can't You See"

1976 - "Are You Ready for the Country"

1977 - "Luckenbach, Texas (Back to the Basics of Love)"

1977 - "The Wurlitzer Prize (I Don't Want to Get Over You)"

1978 - "I've Always Been Crazy"

1978 - "Don't You Think This Outlaw Bit's Done Got Out of Hand"

1979 - "Amanda"

1979 - "Come with Me"

1979 - "I Ain't Living Long Like This"

1980 - "Clyde"

1980 - "Theme from The Dukes of Hazzard (Good Ol' Boys)"

1981 - "Shine"

1982 - "Women Do Know How to Carry On"

1983 - "Lucille (You Won't Do Your Daddy's Will)"

1983 - "Breakin' Down"

1983 - "Hold On, I'm Comin'" (with Jerry Reed)

1983 - "The Conversation" (with Hank Williams, Jr.)

1984 - "I May Be Used (But Baby I Ain't Used Up)"

1984 - "Never Could Toe the Mark"

1984 - "America"

1985 - "Waltz Me to Heaven"

1985 - "Drinkin' and Dreamin'"

1985 - "The Devil's on the Loose"

1986 - "Working Without a Net"

1986 - "Will the Wolf Survive"

1986 - "What You'll Do When I'm Gone"

1987 - "Rose in Paradise"

1987 - "Fallin' Out"

1987 - "Rough and Rowdy Days"

1988 - "If Ole Hank Could Only See Us Now"

1988 - "How Much Is It Worth to Live in L.A."

1989 - "Which Way Do I Go (Now That I'm Gone)"

1989 - "Trouble Man"

1989 - "You Put the Soul in the Song"

1990 - "Wrong"

1990 - "Where Corn Don't Grow"

1990 - "What Bothers Me Most"

1991 - "The Eagle"

1992 - "Just Talkin'"

1992 - "Too Dumb for New York City"

1998 - "I Know About Me, I Don't Know About You"

2012 - "Goin' Down Rockin'"

OTHER SINGLES

Singles with Jessi Colter

1970 - "Suspicious Minds"

1971 - "Under Your Spell Again"

1976 - "Suspicious Minds" (re-release)

1981 - "Storms Never Last"

1981 - "The Wild Side of Life/It Wasn't God Who Made Honky Tonk Angels"

1996 - "Deep in the West"

Singles with Willie Nelson

1976 - "Good Hearted Woman" (re-recording)

1978 - "Mammas Don't Let Your Babies Grow Up to Be Cowboys"

1982 - "Just to Satisfy You"

1982 - "(Sittin' On) The Dock of the Bay"

1983 - "Take It to the Limit"

1991 - "If I Can Find a Clean Shirt"

1991 - "Tryin' to Outrun the Wind"

Other collaborations

1969 - "MacArthur Park" The Kimberlys

1986 - "Even Cowgirls Get the Blues" Johnny Cash

1986 - "The Ballad of Forty Dollars" Johnny Cash

GUEST SINGLES

1967 - "Chet's Tune" Some of Chet's Friends

1978 - "There Ain't No Good Chain Gang" Johnny Cash

1983 - "Leave Them Boys Alone" Hank Williams, Jr. (with Ernest Tubb)

1985 - "We Are the World" USA for Africa

1988 - "Somewhere Between Ragged and Right" John Anderson

1988 - "High Ridin' Heroes" David Lynn Jones

1996 - "One Good Love"   Neil Diamond

1999 - "Still Gonna Die" Old Dogs

.

Made in the USA
Columbia, SC
05 June 2021